Liquid

Liquid Surveillance

A Conversation

Zygmunt Bauman and David Lyon

polity

First published in 2013 by Polity Press

Polity Press
65 Bridge Street
Cambridge CB2 1UR, UK

Polity Press
350 Main Street
Malden, MA 02148, USA

ISBN-13: 978-0-7456-6282-4
ISBN-13: 978-0-7456-6283-1(pb)

A catalogue record for this book is available from the British Library.

Typeset in 11 on 14pt Sabon
by Servis Filmsetting Ltd, Stockport, Cheshire
Printed and bound in Great Britain by the MPG Books Group

For further information on Polity, visit our website: www.politybooks.com

Contents

Preface and acknowledgements

Surveillance is a growing feature of daily news, reflecting its rapid rise to prominence in many life spheres. But in fact surveillance has been expanding quietly for many decades and is a basic feature of the modern world. As that world has transformed itself through successive generations, so surveillance takes on an ever changing character. Today, modern societies seem so fluid that it makes sense to think of them being in a 'liquid' phase. Always on the move, but often lacking certainty and lasting bonds, today's citizens, workers, consumers and travellers also find that their movements are monitored, tracked and traced. Surveillance slips into a liquid state.

This book examines through conversation how far the notion of liquid surveillance helps us grasp what is happening in the world of monitoring, tracking, tracing, sorting, checking and systematic watching that we call surveillance. This provides the key thread through our conversation. It engages with both historical debates over the panopticon design for surveillance as well as contemporary developments in a globalized gaze that seems to leave nowhere to hide, and simultaneously is welcomed as such. But it also stretches outwards to touch large questions sometimes unreached by debates over surveillance. It is a conversation in which each participant contributes more or less equally to the whole.

The two of us have been in touch, discussing sporadically issues of new technologies, surveillance, sociology and social theory since the late 1970s (or early 1980s, we can't recall). Bauman has continued to use the panopticon critique and related themes in his work and has encouraged Lyon in his growing analysis of surveillance. Most recently, we prepared back-to-back presentations for the Surveillance Studies Network biannual conference in 2008 (Bauman's had to be given *in absentia*). Lyon's was published in *International Political Sociology* (Dec. 2010) as 'Liquid surveillance: the contribution of Zygmunt Bauman's work to surveillance studies'. Bauman's contribution to that event is unpublished. Our conversation occurred by email between September and November 2011.

We're very grateful for the very thoughtful help given by some valued colleagues in reading our conversation and making suggestions for how things might be better put, and made more accessible to a wider audience: Katja Franko Aas, Kirstie Ball, Will Katerberg, Keith Tester. Warm thanks are also due to Emily Smith, Research Associate at the Surveillance Studies Centre at Queen's University, Canada for help with this project, and Andrea Drugan, our Polity editor, and Ann Bone, copy-editor, for their encouragement and advice.

Zygmunt Bauman and David Lyon

Introduction

David Lyon Surveillance is a key dimension of the modern world and in most countries people are all too aware of how surveillance affects them. Not only in London and New York but also in New Delhi, Shanghai and Rio de Janeiro video cameras are a familiar sight in public places. Travellers through airports everywhere are conscious that they not only have to negotiate twentieth-century passport control but also newer devices such as body scanners and biometric checks that have proliferated since 9/11. And if these have to do with security, other kinds of surveillance, relating to routine and mundane purchases or online access or participation in social media, are also increasingly ubiquitous. We have to show ID, insert passwords and use coded controls in numerous contexts from making online purchases to entering buildings. Every day, Google notes our searches, prompting customized marketing strategies.

But what does this mean, socially, culturally, politically? If we simply start with new technologies or regulatory regimes we may acquire some sense of the scope of this phenomenon but will we understand it? Certainly, getting an idea of the magnitude and rapid spread of data processing is vital if the surveillance surge is to be appreciated for what it is, and discovering just whose life chances and opportunities are affected by surveillance will galvanize efforts to rein it in. But this conversation is intended to do more, to dig deeper – to probe the historical and Western origins of today's surveillance and to raise ethical as well as political queries about its expansion.

Surveillance has been a constant theme of Zygmunt Bauman's work over several decades and many of his observations are, in my view, of great interest to those trying to understand and respond to surveillance today. In the first decade of the twenty-first century Bauman became best known for his reflections on the rise of 'liquid modernity' and here we explore how far this frame is also illuminating for considering the contemporary role of surveillance. But the other leitmotif of Bauman's analysis is the stress on ethics, above all the ethics of the Other. To what extent does this offer a critical handle on surveillance today?

Liquid surveillance?

'Liquid surveillance' is less a complete way of specifying surveillance and more an orientation, a way of situating surveillance developments in the fluid and unsettling modernity of today. Surveillance softens especially in the consumer realm. Old moorings are loosened as bits of personal data extracted for one purpose are more easily deployed in another. Surveillance spreads in hitherto unimaginable ways, responding to and reproducing liquidity. Without a fixed container, but jolted by 'security' demands and tipped by technology companies' insistent marketing, surveillance spills out all over. Bauman's notion of liquid modernity frames surveillance in new ways and offers both striking insights into why surveillance develops the way it does and some productive ideas on how its worst effects might be confronted and countered. Of course, that's my view of the situation. What Zygmunt Bauman thinks becomes clear in our conversation . . .

It is widely accepted that surveillance is a central dimension of modernity. But modernity does not stand still. We also have to ask, what *sort* of modernity? Today's conditions may be described as 'late' modernity, possibly 'postmodernity' or, more colourfully, as 'liquid' modernity. Zygmunt Bauman suggests that modernity has *liquefied* in some new and different ways (beyond Marx and Engels's early modern insight that 'all that is solid melts into air'). Two features stand out.

First, all social forms melt faster than new ones can be cast. They cannot hold their shape or solidify into frames of reference for human actions and life strategies because of their short shelf-life. Does this apply to surveillance? A number of theorists have noted the ways in which surveillance, once seemingly solid and fixed, has become much more flexible and mobile, seeping and spreading into many life areas where once it had only marginal sway.

Gilles Deleuze introduced the 'society of control' where surveillance grows less like a tree – relatively rigid, in a vertical plane, like the panopticon – and more like creeping weeds.[1] As Haggerty and Ericson observe, following this, the 'surveillant assemblage' captures flows of what we might call body data, turning them into highly fluid and mobile 'data doubles'.[2] William Staples also notes that today's surveillance occurs in cultures 'characterized by fragmentation and uncertainty as many of the once-taken-for-granted meanings, symbols and institutions of modern life *dissolve* before our eyes'.[3] Thus the bounded, structured and stable liquefies.

Bauman agrees that the panopticon was a key modern means of keeping control, by barring movement among inmates and promoting it among the watchers. But the watchers still had to be present sometimes. Of course the prison panopticon project was also expensive. It was designed to facilitate control through a semi-circular arrangement of cell blocks whose 'inspector' at the centre could see into any cell while remaining invisible to the inmates, behind a blind. It entailed the inspector taking some responsibility for the lives of inmates. Today's world, says Bauman, is post-panoptical.[4] The inspectors can slip away, escaping to unreachable realms. Mutual engagement is over. Mobility and nomadism are now prized (unless you're poor or homeless). The smaller, lighter, faster is seen as good – at least in the world of iPhones and iPads.

The panopticon is just one model of surveillance.[5] The architecture of electronic technologies through which power is asserted in today's mutable and mobile organizations makes the architecture of walls and windows largely redundant (virtual 'firewalls' and 'windows' notwithstanding). And it permits forms of control that display different faces. Not only do they have no obvious connection with imprisonment, they often share the features of flexibility and fun seen in entertainment and consumption. Airport check-in can be done with a smartphone, even though the international exchanges involving the crucial PNR (passenger name record) still occur, prompted by the original reservation (which itself could have been generated on that smartphone).

Discipline and security are actually related, in this view, something that Foucault failed to recognize. Foucault insisted on their separation just as their (electronic) connections were becoming clearer. Security has morphed into a future-oriented enterprise – now neatly captured in the *Minority Report* (2002) film and novel – and works through surveillance by attempting to monitor what *will* happen, using digital techniques and statistical reasoning. As Didier Bigo points out, such security operates by tracking '*everything that moves* (products, information, capital, humanity)'.[6] So surveillance works at a distance in both space and time, circulating fluidly with, but beyond, nation-states in a globalized realm. Reassurance and rewards accompany those mobile groups for whom such techniques are made to appear 'natural'. Profiling processes and exclusionary measures await the groups unlucky enough to be labelled 'unwelcome'.

Secondly, and related to this, power and politics are splitting apart. Power now exists in global and extraterritorial space, but politics, which once linked individual and public interests, remains local, unable to act at the planetary level. Without political control, power becomes a source of great uncertainty, while politics seems irrelevant to many people's life problems and fears. Surveillance power, as exercised by government departments, police agencies and private corporations, fits this depiction well. Even national borders, which once had geographical locations – however arbitrary – now appear in airports distant from the 'edge' of the territory and, more significantly, in databases that may not even be 'in' the country in question.[7]

Continuing with this example, the issue of mutable borders is a source of great uncertainty for many. It is an anxious moment to go through airport security, not knowing exactly whose jurisdiction you are in or where your personal details may end up, especially for those who may be part of a suspect population. And if you are unfortunate enough to be detained or to discover that your name is on a no-fly list, knowing what to do is notoriously hard. Beyond this, effecting political change that might, for instance, make necessary travel more straightforward is a daunting challenge.

The melting of social forms and the splitting of power and politics are two key features of liquid modernity that have obvious resonance with surveillance, but it is worth mentioning two further connections. One is the mutual relation between new media and fluid relationships. While some blame new media for social fragmentation, Bauman sees things working both ways. He suggests that social media are a product of social fragmentation, not only – or necessarily – vice versa. He says that in liquid modernity power must be free to flow, and barriers, fences, borders and checkpoints are a nuisance to be overcome or circumvented. Dense and tight networks of social bonds, especially based on territory, must be cleared away. For him, it's the brittleness of those bonds that allows the powers to work in the first place.

Applied to social media, this is controversial, because

many activists see great potential for social solidarity and political organizing in tweets and messaging. Think of the Occupy movement, the widespread protest of the so-called 99 per cent against the privilege and power of the 1 per cent in the world's richest countries, or the Arab Spring, in 2011. However, this is an area to be carefully watched, not least because it is *already* being surveilled. Social media depend for their existence on monitoring users and selling the data to others. The possibilities for social media resistance are attractive and in some ways fruitful, but they are also limited, both due to the lack of resources for binding relationships in a liquefying world and to the fact that surveillance power *within* social media is endemic and consequential.

The final connection to be made here is that liquid times offer some acute challenges for any who would act ethically, not least in the world of surveillance. Bauman's recognition of the uncertainties endemic in a liquid modern world shapes the problem as he sees it. And his favoured stance, spurning lifeless rules and regulations, is seen in his stress on the significance of the lived encounter with the Other. Realizing our responsibility for the human being before us is his starting point.

Two major issues confront surveillance ethics here. One is the distressing tendency towards what Bauman calls 'adiaphorization' in which systems and processes become split off from any consideration of morality.[8] 'It's not my department' would be the quintessential bureaucratic response to queries about the rightness of an official assessment or judgement. The other is that surveillance streamlines the process of doing things at a distance, of separating a person from the consequences of an action. Thus border controls can appear automated, dispassionate, even as they deny entry to the asylum seeker from the 'wrong' ethnic background, fearful for her life if she is sent back home.

Another angle on adiaphorization in surveillance is the way that data from the body (such as biometrics, DNA) or triggered by the body (think of logging in, using access cards, showing ID) are sucked into databases to be processed, analysed, concatenated with other data, then spat out again as a 'data double'. The information that proxies for the person is made up of 'personal data' only in the sense that it originated with a person's body and may affect their life chances and choices. The piecemeal data double tends to be trusted more than the person, who prefers to tell their own tale. Software designers say they're simply 'dealing with data', so their role is 'morally neutral' and their assessments and discrimination are just 'rational'.[9]

Think liquid

So, how far does the notion of liquid modernity – and here, liquid surveillance – help us grasp what is happening in the world of monitoring, tracking, tracing, sorting, checking and systematic watching that is surveillance? The simple one-word response is 'context'. It is easy to read the spread of surveillance as a technological phenomenon or as one that simply speaks of 'social control' and 'Big Brother'. But this puts all the stress on tools and tyrants and ignores the spirit that animates surveillance, the ideologies that drive it forward, the events that give it its chance and the ordinary people who comply with it, question it or who decide that if they can't beat it, they'll join the game.

Popular readings of surveillance conceive these developments as the ever quickening march of technology, colonizing more and more life areas and leaving intact fewer and fewer untouched 'indigenous' areas of 'private' existence. So from the ubiquitous barcode that identifies various classes of product as being of the same kind or from the same plant, we move to radio-frequency identification (RFID) chips that offer unique identifiers for each individual product. But not only products. RFIDs are also used in passports and clothing and their emitted data can easily be connected with the bearer or the wearer. At the same time, other devices, such as QR (quick response) codes, squares of chequered symbols that can be scanned with a smartphone, appear on many products, signs and, yes, on clothing (though they too originated in the quest for accelerated supply chains). Wear a silicone bracelet with a QR as a fashion accessory and just whisper 'scan me'. This pulls up a web page with your contact details, social media links and the rest. You are a human hyperlink.

Dwellers in the world of 'solid' modernity would recognize and maybe applaud the idea of barcodes as being an efficient way of cataloguing inventory. Behold bureaucratic rationalization perfectly expressed in a technological device. But the RFID tag speaks more of a world in which greater attention must be paid, not merely to classifying and selling products, but also to finding out exactly where they are at any given moment within a just-in-time management regime. Mere inventory is waste. You need *kanban* (as the Japanese call them) to signal that the right thing is in the right place at the right time. No wonder the idea works so transferably in the security world!

But while in the solid modern world some would have approved the notion of knowing personal details to ensure that the right people are in the right place at the right time, who would have imagined (in a solidly modern world) that such details would willingly be advertised to all and sundry? While RFID suits situations where data are constantly required, new QR applications speak to a world where people are actively engaged in data sharing. RFID, for instance, checks the flows across borders, filtering them to permit the easy passage of some goods and persons but not others. But the new QR, while it is still surveillant, aims to minimize the friction of consumption by freely sharing information about events, opportunities and, possibly, persons. Its appeal reflects its liquid modern context.

What about the question of social control, of George Orwell's Big Brother? If surveillance is not just about the growing grip of new technologies, then isn't it about the way that power is distributed? The key metaphor for surveillance, in the Western world at least, is undoubtedly Big Brother. When government administration becomes focused in the hands of a single person or party, using the administrative apparatus with its files and records as a means of complete control, we speak of Big Brother. In Orwell's *1984* – as I once put it – 'intended as a post World War II warning about the totalitarian potentiality of Western democracies, the state has become pathologically absorbed with its own power and is intimately involved in everyday control of its citizens' lives'.[10]

But while Orwell's metaphor is compelling (and his own commitment to human 'decency' as its antidote equally so), there are others. Franz Kafka's description of shadowy powers that leave you uncertain of anything (Who knows what about you? How do they know? How will this knowledge affect you?) is perhaps closer to the mark in today's database world (as Daniel Solove and others have argued)[11] but, like Orwell's, it still refers primarily to agents of the state. A somewhat earlier metaphor comes from the English utilitarian prison reformer Jeremy Bentham, with a name cobbled from Greek to make 'panopticon', for 'all-seeing place'. But his was no fiction. It was a plan, a diagram, an architect's drawing. And it was more. It was meant as 'moral architecture', a recipe for remaking the world.

It is this postulate, panopticon, that most extensively connects the world of scholarship with surveillance, not just because of Bentham, but because of Michel Foucault, who in the mid-twentieth century saw in it the centrepiece of what Bauman calls solid modernity. Foucault focused on panoptic discipline, or 'soul training', producing willing workers. For Bauman, Foucault uses panopticon as the 'arch-metaphor of modern power'. The prisoners in the panopticon 'could not move because they were all under watch; they had to stick to their appointed places at all times because they did not know, and had no way of knowing, where at the moment the watchers – free to move at will – were'.[12] Today, however, such rigid fixity is dissolved such that (whether or not we call this stage of modernity 'liquid') 'it is also, perhaps above all, *post-panoptical*'. If then it could be assumed that the panopticon inspector was present (somewhere), in today's power relations those holding the levers of power 'can at any moment escape beyond reach – into sheer inaccessibility'.[13]

Both Bauman and I think (not necessarily for the

same reasons!) that much hangs on the fate of the panopticon, and part of our project here is to tease out the very pressing and practical implications of what to some may appear to be an abstractly academic debate. Just as the phrase 'Big Brother' continues to capture the imagination of those bothered about overbearing state powers, so the portrayal of the panopticon tells us much about how surveillance operates in the twenty-first century. If Bauman is right, then the curtain has dropped on the era of 'mutual engagement' in which managers and managed confronted each other: the new show is a more elusive drama in which 'power can move with the speed of an electronic signal'.

The challenges presented by this are tremendous. Put very simply, new surveillance practices, based on information processing rather than the discourses that Foucault had in mind,[14] permit a new transparency in which not just citizens but all of us, across the range of roles we play in everyday life, are constantly checked, monitored, tested, assessed, valued and judged. But the converse is clearly not true. As the details of our daily lives become more transparent to the organizations surveilling us, their own activities become less and less easy to discern. As power moves with the speed of electronic signals in the fluidity of liquid modernity, transparency is simultaneously increased for some and decreased for others.

However, this is not necessarily intentional let alone conspiratorial. Part of the opaqueness of new surveillance has to do with its sophisticated technical character and with the complex flows of data within and between organizations. Another part has to do with the secrecy surrounding 'national security' or commercial competition. Moreover, in what Bauman calls the post-panoptical world of liquid modernity much of the personal information vacuumed so vigorously by organizations is actually made available by people using their cellphones, shopping in malls, travelling on vacation, being entertained or surfing the internet. We swipe our cards, repeat our postcodes and show our ID routinely, automatically, willingly.

All of which does not, however, let us off the hook. Because just as there were profound social and political consequences of modern panopticism, so such consequences still attend the largely post-panoptical powers of liquid modernity. And while loss of privacy might be the first thing that springs to many minds when surveillance is in question, arguably privacy is not the most significant casualty. The issues of anonymity, confidentiality and privacy should not be ignored, but they are also bound up with those of fairness and justice, civil liberties and human rights. This is because, as we shall see, *social sorting* is primarily what today's surveillance achieves, for better or for worse.[15]

There are of course some continuities between older and newer forms of surveillance power; each serves to distribute life chances, opportunities, rewards and privilege. Panoptic principles served historically to maintain hierarchy and class distinctions, in homes and schools as well as in factories and prisons.[16] So while paradoxically the currents and eddies of today's liquid modernity may appear arbitrary and haphazard, the logic of statistics and software that drives today's surveillance produces outcomes that are uncannily consistent. Not merely – and egregiously – do 'Arabs' and 'Muslims' find that they are subject to far more 'random' scrutiny than others at airports, but also, as Oscar Gandy demonstrates, the social sorting achieved by contemporary consumer surveillance constructs a world of 'cumulative disadvantage'.[17]

But we're getting ahead of ourselves. I suggest that the concept of liquid modernity offers a broader context within which to consider surveillance than merely the growth of technologies or the growing grasp of power. Surveillance, which took its place as a key social institution only in modern times, now shares some features with and is shaped by the emerging forms of modernity dubbed 'liquid' by Bauman. Thus one way to get a handle on the nascent patterns of surveillance is to explore how they relate to liquid modernity.

Conversing together

The conversations that follow consider a range of tensions and paradoxes in contemporary surveillance, using the 'liquid' metaphor described above as a probe. We begin the journey, as it were, right where we are, in the world of electronically mediated relationships. Bauman published a typically ironic piece in the summer of 2011, 'On never being alone again', that mused on surveillance drones and social media, and this topic will get us right into the subject matter. The drones can now be as tiny as hummingbirds but the nectar they seek is increasingly high resolution images of those in their path. But why would we care, anyway? After all, anonymity is already being auto-eroded on Facebook and on other social media. The private is public, to be celebrated and consumed by countless 'friends' as well as casual 'users'.

As we've already hinted, however, we cannot evade the question of the post-panoptic dimensions of liquid modernity and we shall delve right into this debate. It situates our discussion by contrasting the fixity and spatial orientation of solid modern surveillance with the mobile, pulsating signals of today's flowing forms. At what points should we continue to follow Foucault and where does his account need updating, expanding or, for that matter, repudiating? These conversations will weave together related threads, too: on the relation of metaphor and concept, on debates with the likes of Deleuze, Derrida and Agamben, and of course on the political and ethical repercussions of our theoretical and conceptual choices.

The technological, or rather the techno-social, dimensions of today's surveillance will also be on the table and again we'll reach back to recall those dreadfully ambivalent legacies of solid modernity exposed by Bauman in *Modernity and the Holocaust* (2001). Could it be that the meticulous organization, the careful separation of the official from the victim, and the mechanical efficiency of the operation seen in the human cattle trains and death camps are now devoted, not to physical violence, but to the sorting of populations into categories for differential treatment? How do electronic and networked technologies achieve these less cataclysmic but not much less insidious consequences, particularly for already marginalized groups? Remoteness, distancing and automation each play their computer-assisted part today.

A further conversation thread concerns those forms of surveillance relating specifically to security. In the global north, 9/11 serves to amplify already-existing obsessions with security and risk, even if the events of 9/11 are read quite differently around the world. We'll eschew the simplistic notions that civil liberties and security exist in a zero-sum game or that only those with 'something to hide' have anything to fear. And we'll send our sonar to sound out the emerging security-surveillance complex in which outsourcing and contract procurement draw together the data-dredging worlds of commerce and intelligence agencies, and in which the classic weapons of fear and suspicion are still wielded.

And in case you were wondering what has happened to the classic Baumanian themes of consumerism and the reproduction of poverty,[18] before our coffee is cold we'll confront that too, querying all the while its significant surveillance dimensions. Bauman has tirelessly exposed the ways in which consumerism is symbiotic with the production of social divisions and also social identities. A paradox here is that while consumption entails the pleasurable seduction of consumers, such seduction is also the result of systematic surveillance on a massive scale. If this was not obvious through previous forms of database marketing, the advent of Amazon, Facebook and Google indicates the current state of the art. But once again, that's to anticipate.

Each theme of this conversation raises questions not only about the appropriate analysis of surveillance – Is it liquid? What difference does this make? – but also about the insistent ethical challenges accompanying such analysis. Picking up from some analysis in Bauman's *Postmodern Ethics* (1993) and elsewhere, we'll ask how far disclosive or even normative ethics might speak to the realities of contemporary surveillance. How far can these be used in addressing today's urgent political realities of surveillance, whether in demands from government for unlimited access to personal data from internet service providers, or in the use of health profiles to withhold insurance coverage from some patients?

The last conversation, on 'agency and hope', does take us well beyond liquid surveillance (actually, the previous conversations do as well; we could hardly help ourselves!). But these issues have resurfaced several times in earlier talks so we tried to face them head-on here. I must confess that as our transatlantic talks built up to this point, I found them more and more exhilarating – not to say electrifying – and found it hard to wait for the responses. At the same time, when they came (faster than mine, it must be said), I sometimes puzzled over how we had reached this point in the conversation! I think that, frankly, there are some things that my dear friend really wants to say while there are others that, press him as I might, he'd rather not. And that's just fine. I respect him the more for it.

In all this dialogue it should be stressed that we're simply exploring together, sharing ideas and insights, prompted by the overarching conviction that the liquid modernity theorem offers some vital clues for considering surveillance today. But while we're in accord over some crucial common commitments, we don't agree on a number of weighty points. However, we do agree that they're worth discussing, too.

I
Drones and social media

David Lyon   With those introductory comments about liquid surveillance in mind, the first question I'd like us to explore is this: In what you call a liquid modern world, surveillance morphs into some significant new forms, of which drones and social media offer fine examples, as you noted in a blog post recently. Each produces personal information for processing, but in different ways. Are these media complementary, such that the blithe use of one (social media) naturalizes us to the more unwitting extraction of personal data in another field by means of miniaturizing drones? And what do these new developments mean for our anonymity and relative invisibility in the everyday world?

Zygmunt Bauman   I guess the little piece which you mention, published a few months ago in a blog post on the Social Europe website, would be a good point to start; I hope you'll forgive my quoting it at length. In that essay I juxtaposed two apparently unconnected items of news that appeared on the same day, 19 June

2011 – though neither of them made headlines and readers could be forgiven for overlooking one of them or both. Like any news, the two items were carried in by the daily 'information tsunami': just two tiny drops in a flood of news ostensibly meant and hoped to do the job of enlightening and clarifying, while serving to obscure the vision and befuddle the looking . . .

One item of news, authored by Elisabeth Bumiller and Thom Shanker,[19] told of the spectacular rise in the number of drones reduced to the size of a dragonfly, or of a hummingbird comfortably perching on windowsills; both designed, in the juicy expression of Greg Parker, an aerospace engineer, 'to hide in plain sight'. The second, penned by Brian Stelter, proclaimed the internet to be 'the place where anonymity dies'.[20] The two messages spoke in unison, they both augured and portended the end of invisibility and autonomy, the two defining attributes of privacy – even though each of the two items was composed independently of the other and without awareness of the other's existence.

The unmanned drones, performing the spying and striking tasks for which the Predators have become notorious ('More than 1,900 insurgents in Pakistan's tribal areas have been killed by American drones since 2006'), are about to be shrunk to the size of birds, but preferably insects (the flapping of insects' wings is ostensibly much easier to imitate technologically than the movements of birds' wings and, according to Major Michael L. Anderson, a doctoral student in advanced navigation technology, the exquisite aerodynamic skills of the hawk moth, an insect known for its hovering skills, have been selected as a target of the present designing flurry – not yet attained, but certain to be reached soon – because of its potential to leave far behind anything 'our clumsy aircraft can do').

The new generation of drones will stay invisible while making everything else accessible to be viewed; they will stay immune while rendering everything else vulnerable. In the words of Peter Baker, an ethics professor at the United States Naval Academy, those drones will usher wars into the 'post-heroic age'; but they will also, according to other 'military ethicists', widen still further the already vast 'disconnect between the American public and its war'; they will perform, in other words, another leap (the second after the replacement of the conscript by a professional army) towards making the war itself all but invisible to the nation in whose name the war is waged (no native lives will be at risk) and so that much easier – indeed so much more tempting – to conduct, thanks to the almost complete absence of collateral damage and political costs.

The next-generation drones will see all while staying comfortably invisible – literally as well as metaphorically. There will be no shelter from being spied on – for anyone. Even the technicians who send drones into action will renounce control over their movements and so become unable, however strongly pressed, to exempt any object from the chance of falling under surveillance: the 'new and improved' drones will be programmed to fly on their own, following itineraries of their own choice at times of their own choice. The sky is the limit for the information they will supply once they are put into operation in the numbers planned.

This is, as a matter of fact, the aspect of the new spying and surveilling technology, armed as it is with the capacity to act at a distance and autonomously, that most worries its designers, and as a result the two news writers reporting their preoccupations: 'a tsunami of data', which is already overwhelming the staff at Air Force headquarters and threatening to outrun their powers to digest and absorb it, and thus also to run out of their (or anybody else's) control. Since 9/11, the number of hours needed by Air Force employees in order to recycle the intelligence supplied by the drones went up by 3,100 per cent – and each day 1,500 more hours of videos are added to the volume of information clamouring to be processed. Once the limited 'soda straw' view of drone sensors is replaced with a 'Gorgon stare' able to embrace a whole city in one go (an imminent development), 2,000 analysts will be required to cope with the feeds of just one drone, instead of the nineteen analysts doing the job today. But that only means, let me comment, that fishing out an 'interesting', 'relevant' object from the bottomless container of 'data' will take some hard work and cost rather a lot of money; not that any of the potentially interesting objects could insure themselves against being swept into that container in the first place. No one will ever know for sure whether or when a hummingbird might land on his or her windowsill.

As for the 'death of anonymity' courtesy of the internet, the story is slightly different: we submit our rights to privacy for slaughter of our own will. Or perhaps we just consent to the loss of privacy as a reasonable price for the wonders offered in exchange. Or the pressure to deliver our personal autonomy to the slaughterhouse is so overwhelming, so close to the condition of a flock of sheep, that only a few exceptionally rebellious, bold, pugnacious and resolute wills are prepared to make an earnest attempt to withstand it. One way or another, however, we are offered, at least nominally, a choice, as well as at least a semblance of a two-way contract, and at least a formal right to protest and sue in the event it is breached: something never granted in the case of drones.

All the same, once we are in, we stay hostages to fate. As Brian Stelter observes, 'the collective intelligence of the Internet's two billion users, and the digital finger-prints that so many users leave on Web sites, combine to make it more and more likely that every embarrassing video, every intimate photo, and every indelicate e-mail is attributed to its source, whether that source wants it to be or not'. It took Rich Lam, a freelance photographer taking pictures of street riots in Vancouver, just one day to trace and identify a couple caught on one of his photos (by accident) passionately kissing. Everything private is now done, potentially, in public – and is potentially available for public consumption; and remains avail-able for the duration, till the end of time, as the internet 'can't be made to forget' anything once recorded on any of its innumerable servers. 'This erosion of anonymity is a product of pervasive social media services, cheap cell phone cameras, free photo and video Web hosts, and perhaps most important of all, a change in people's views about what ought to be public and what ought to be private.' All those technical gadgets are, we are told, 'user friendly' – though that favourite phrase of commer-cial copy means, under closer scrutiny, a product that is incomplete without the user's labour, along the lines of IKEA furniture. And, let me add, without users' enthusi-astic devotion and deafening applause. A contemporary Étienne de la Boétie would probably be tempted to speak not of a voluntary, but a DIY servitude . . .

What conclusion can be drawn from that meeting between the drone operators and the Facebook accounts operators? Between the two kinds of operators acting apparently at cross-purposes and activated by ostensibly opposite motives, yet nonetheless cooperating closely, willingly and highly effectively in bringing about, sustaining and expanding what you have, so felicitously, dubbed 'social sorting'? I believe that the most remarkable feature of the contemporary edition of surveillance is that it has somehow managed to force and cajole oppositions to work in unison, and to make them work in concert in the service of the same reality. On the one hand, the old panoptical stratagem ('you should never know when you are being watched in the flesh and so never be unwatched in your mind') is being gradually yet consistently and apparently unstoppably brought to well-nigh universal implementation. On the other, with the old panoptical nightmare ('I am never on my own') now recast into the hope of 'never again being alone' (abandoned, ignored and neglected, blackballed and excluded), the fear of disclosure has been stifled by the joy of being noticed.

The two developments, and above all their reconciliation and cooperation in promoting the same task, were of course made possible by exclusion being substituted for incarceration and confinement in the role of the most awesome threat to existential security and the major source of anxiety. The condition of being watched and seen has thereby been reclassified from a menace into a temptation. The promise of enhanced visibility, the prospect of 'being in the open' for everybody to see and everybody to notice, chimes well with the most avidly sought proof of social recognition, and therefore of valued – 'meaningful' – existence. Having one's own complete being, warts and all, registered in publicly accessible records seems to be the best prophylactic antidote against the toxicity of exclusion – as well as a potent way to keep the threat of eviction away; indeed, it is a temptation few practitioners of admittedly precarious social existence will feel strong enough to resist. I guess that the story of the recent phenomenal success of 'social websites' is a good illustration of the trend.

Indeed, the twenty-year-old Harvard dropout Mark Zuckerberg must have stumbled on some kind of a goldmine, in inventing (some people say stealing)[21] the Facebook idea – and launching it, for the exclusive use of Harvard students, on the internet in February 2004. That much is pretty obvious. But what was that gold-like ore that lucky Mark discovered and goes on mining with fabulous, and still steadily rising, profits?

On the official Facebook site you can find the following description of the benefits credited with tempting, attracting and seducing all those half-billion people to spend a good deal of their waking time on Facebook's virtual expanses:

> Users can create profiles with photos, lists of personal interests, contact information, and other personal information. Users can communicate with friends and other users through private or public messages and a chat feature. They can also create and join interest groups and 'like pages' (formerly called 'fan pages', until April 19, 2010), some of which are maintained by organizations as a means of advertising.

In other words, what the legions of 'active users' enthusiastically embraced when they joined the ranks of

Facebook 'active users' was the prospect of two things they must have been dreaming of, yet without knowing where to seek or find them, before (and until) Mark Zuckerberg's offer to his fellow students in Harvard appeared on the internet. First, they must have felt too lonely for comfort, but found it too difficult for one reason or another to escape their loneliness with the means at their disposal. Second, they must have felt painfully neglected, unnoticed, ignored and otherwise shuttled on to a side-track, exiled and excluded, but once again found it difficult, nay impossible, to lift themselves out of their hateful anonymity with the means at their disposal. For both tasks, Zuckerberg offered the means they had hitherto found terribly missing and sought for in vain; and they jumped at the opportunity. They must have been ready to jump, feet already in the starting blocks, muscles tensed, ears pricked for the starter's shot.

As Josh Rose, the digital creative director of ad agency Deutsch LA, has recently observed, 'The Internet doesn't steal our humanity, it reflects it. The Internet doesn't get inside us, it shows what's inside us.'[22] How right he is. Never blame the messenger for what you found to be bad in the message he delivered, but do not praise him either for what you found to be good . . . It depends, after all, on the recipients' own likings and animosities, dreams and nightmares, hopes and apprehensions, whether they'd rejoice or despair at the message. What applies to messages and messengers applies in certain ways to the things the internet offers and its 'messengers' – the people who display them on our screens and bring them to our attention. In this case, it is the uses that we – Facebook's 'active users', all half-billion of us – make of those offers that render them, and their impact on our lives, good or bad, beneficial or harmful. It all depends on what we are after; technical gadgets just make our longings more or less realistic and our search faster or slower, more or less effective.

DL Yes, I too appreciate the emphasis on what the use of the internet and social media reveals about our social relationships, not least because this gives us clues about what is changing. Questions of 'privacy', for instance, are in flux and are much more complex than was once imagined. We see something similar in the connection of privacy with secrecy, the latter being an important theme in Georg Simmel's sociological classic.[23] For Simmel, not divulging information is crucial to shaping social interaction; how we relate to others depends deeply on what we know about them. But Simmel's article was first published in English in 1906 and the discussion needs updating not only for the ways information flows are facilitated, blocked and diverted today,[24] but also for the renewed challenges in terms of the 'secrets' that exist and their impact in the public domains of social media.

By the later twentieth century, Foucault's ideas on 'confession' became well known. He thought that confession – say, of a crime – had become a key criterion of truth, something pulled up from the depths of someone's being. He noted both the very private means of confession, for instance to a priest, and the public ones that make the headlines. As Foucault understood it, the religious confession was literally 'good for the soul', while its contemporary secular counterparts have personal health and well-being at their heart. Either way, thought Foucault, individuals take an active role in their own surveillance. Now, whether or not Foucault would have thought of the gut-spilling blog or the 'intimate' Facebook post as confessional is a matter for debate. And what is 'public' and what 'private' must be at issue. The Christian confession, whispered to one person, is about humility. The blog is broadcast to anyone who chooses to read it and it is self-advertising. It is about publicity, or at least publicness.

ZB There is a deep difference between the premodern (medieval) understanding of confession – as first and foremost an admission of guilt for something already known, in advance, to the torturers, bodily or spiritual, who extricated it as a restatement and reconfirmation of verity as an attribute of the pastoral superiors – and its modern understanding, as the manifestation, externalization and assertion of an 'inner truth', of the authenticity of the 'self', the foundation of individuality and the individual's privacy. In practice, however, the advent of the present-day confessional society was an ambivalent affair. It signalled the ultimate triumph of privacy, that foremost modern invention – though also the beginning of its vertiginous fall from the peak of its glory. It was the hour, therefore, of its victory (Pyrrhic, to be sure): privacy invaded, conquered and colonized the public realm – but at the expense of losing its right to secrecy: its defining trait and most cherished and most hotly defended privilege.

A secret, like other categories of personal possessions, is by definition that part of knowledge whose sharing with others is refused or prohibited and/or closely controlled. Secrecy draws and marks, as it were, the boundary of privacy – privacy being the realm that is meant to be one's own domain, the territory of one's undivided sovereignty, inside which one has the comprehensive and indivisible power to decide 'what and who I am', and from which one can launch and relaunch the campaign to have and keep one's decisions recognized and respected. In a startling U-turn from the habits of our ancestors, however, we've lost the guts, the stamina, and above all the will to persist in the defence of such rights, those irreplaceable building blocks of individual autonomy.

These days, it is not so much the possibility of a betrayal or violation of privacy that frightens us, but the opposite: shutting down the exits. The area of privacy turns into a site of incarceration, the owner of private space being condemned and doomed to stew in his or her own juice; forced into a condition marked by an absence of avid listeners eager to wring out and tear away the secrets from behind the ramparts of privacy, to put them on public display and make them everybody's shared property and a property everybody wishes to share. *We seem to experience no joy in having secrets*, unless they are the kinds of secrets likely to enhance our egos by attracting the attention of researchers and editors of TV talk shows, tabloid front pages and the covers of glossy magazines.

'At the heart of social networking is an exchange of personal information.' Users are happy to 'reveal intimate details of their personal lives', 'to post accurate information' and 'to share photographs'. It is estimated that 61 per cent of UK teenagers aged 13 to 17 'have a personal profile on a networking site' enabling 'socializing online'.[25]

In Britain, a place where the popular use of cutting-edge electronic facilities lags cyberyears behind East Asia, users may still trust 'social networking' to manifest their freedom of choice, and even believe it to be a means of youthful rebellion and self-assertion. But in South Korea, for instance, where most of social life is already routinely electronically mediated (or rather where *social* life has already turned into an *electronic* life or *cyber*life, and where most 'social life' is conducted primarily in the company of a computer, iPod or mobile, and only secondarily with other fleshy beings), it is obvious to the young that they don't have so much as a sniff of choice; where they live, living social life electronically is no longer a choice but a 'take it or leave it' necessity. 'Social death' awaits those few who have as yet failed to link into Cyworld, South Korea's cybermarket leader in the 'show-and-tell culture'.

It would be a grave mistake, however, to suppose that the urge towards public display of the 'inner self' and the willingness to satisfy that urge are manifestations only of a purely generational, age-related addiction of teenagers, keen as they naturally tend to be to get a foothold in the 'network' (a term rapidly replacing 'society' in both social-scientific discourse and popular speech) and to stay there, while being not quite sure how best to achieve that goal. The new penchant for public confession cannot be explained by 'age-specific' factors – at any rate not *only* by them. As Eugène Enriquez recently summed up the message derived from fast growing evidence, gathered from all sectors of the liquid modern world of consumers,

Provided it is not forgotten that what had previously been invisible – everybody's share of the intimate, everybody's inner life – is now required to be exposed on the public stage (principally on TV screens but also on the literary stage), it can be understood that those who care about their invisibility are bound to be rejected, pushed aside, or suspected of a crime. Physical, social and psychical nudity is the order of the day.[26]

The teenagers equipped with portable electronic confessionals are but apprentices training and trained in the art of living in a confessional society – a society notorious for effacing the boundary that once separated the private from the public, for making public exposure of the private a public virtue and obligation, and for wiping out from public communication anything that resists being reduced to private confidences, together with those who refuse to confide them.

As early as the late 1920s, when the imminent transformation of the society of producers into a society of consumers was in an embryonic or at best incipient stage and so was overlooked by less attentive and far-sighted observers, a comment was made by Siegfried Kracauer, a thinker endowed with an uncanny capacity for gleaning the barely visible and still inchoate contours of the future-prefiguring trends lost in a formless mass of fleeting fads and foibles:

The rush to the numerous beauty salons springs partly from existential concerns, and the use of cosmetic products is not always a luxury. For fear of being withdrawn from use as obsolete, ladies and gentlemen dye their hair, while forty-year-olds take up sports to keep slim. 'How can I become beautiful', runs the title of a booklet recently launched on to the market; the newspaper advertisements for it say that it shows ways 'to stay young and beautiful both now and forever'.[27]

The emergent habits recorded by Kracauer in the early 1920s as a noteworthy Berlin curiosity have spread like a forest fire since then, turning into a daily routine (or at least into a dream) all around the globe. Eighty years later Germaine Greer observed that 'even in the furthest reaches of north-western China, women laid aside their pyjama suits for padded bras and flirty skirts, curled and coloured their straight hair and saved up to buy cosmetics. This was called liberalization.'[28]

Schoolgirls and schoolboys avidly and enthusiastically putting their qualities on display in the hope of capturing attention and possibly also gaining the recognition and approval needed to stay in the game of socializing, prospective clients having to amplify their spending records and credit limits to earn a better service, would-be immigrants struggling to gather and supply brownie points as evidence of a demand for their services in order to have their applications approved: all three categories of people, apparently so distinct, and myriads of other categories forced to sell themselves in the commodity market and looking to sell themselves to the highest bidder, are enticed, nudged or forced to promote an attractive and desirable *commodity*, and so to try as hard as they can, using the best means at their disposal, to enhance the market value of the goods they are selling. And the commodities they are prompted to put on the market, promote and sell are *themselves*.

They are simultaneously *promoters of commodities* and the *commodities they promote*. They are, at the same time, the merchandise and their marketing agents, the goods and their travelling salespersons (and let me add that any academics who ever applied for a teaching job or research funds will easily recognize their own predicament in that experience). In whatever bracket they may be filed by the composers of statistical tables, they all inhabit the same social space known under the name of the *market*. Under whatever rubric their preoccupations might be classified by governmental archivists or investigative journalists, the activity in which all of them are engaged (whether by choice or necessity, or most commonly both) is *marketing*. The test they need to pass in order to be admitted to the social prizes they covet demands them *to recast themselves as commodities*: that is, as products capable of drawing attention, and attracting *demand* and *customers*.

'To consume' means nowadays not so much the delights of the palate, as investing in one's own social membership, which in the society of consumers translates as 'saleability': obtaining qualities for which there is already a market demand, or recycling those already possessed into commodities for which demand can still be created. Most consumer commodities on offer in the consumer market derive their attraction and their power to enlist keen customers from their genuine or imputed, explicitly advertised or obliquely implied *investment* value. Their promise to increase the attractiveness, and consequently the market price, of their buyers is written – in large or small print, or at least between the lines – into the description of every product. This includes the products that are ostensibly to be purchased mostly or even exclusively for the sake of pure consumer pleasure. Consumption is an investment in anything that matters for individual 'social value' and self-esteem.

The crucial purpose, perhaps the decisive purpose of consumption in the society of consumers (even if it is seldom spelled out in so many words and even less frequently publicly debated) is not the satisfaction of needs, desires and wants, but the commoditization or recommoditization of the consumer: *raising the status of consumers to that of sellable commodities*. It is ultimately for that reason that the passing of a consumer test is a non-negotiable condition of admission to a society that has been reshaped in the likeness of the marketplace. Passing that test is the *non*-contractual precondition of all the *contractual* relations that weave and are woven into the web of relationships called the 'society of consumers'. It is that precondition, with no exception allowed and no refusal tolerated, that welds the aggregate of seller/buyer transactions into an imagined totality; or which, more exactly, allows that aggregate to be experienced as a totality called 'society' – an entity to which the capacity of 'making demands' and of coercing actors to obey them can be ascribed – enabling the status of the 'social fact' in the Durkheimian sense to be imputed.

Let me repeat: *members of the society of consumers are themselves consumer commodities*, and it is the quality of being a consumer commodity that makes them bona fide members of that society. Becoming and remaining a sellable commodity is the most potent motive of consumer concerns, even though it is usually latent and seldom conscious, let alone explicitly declared. It is by their potency to increase the consumer's market price that the attractiveness of consumer goods

– the current or potential objects of desire triggering consumer action – tends to be evaluated. 'Making oneself a sellable commodity' is a DIY job, and individual duty. Let us note: '*making* oneself', not just *becoming*, is the challenge and the task.

Being a member of the society of consumers is a daunting task and never-ending uphill struggle. The fear of failing to conform has been elbowed out by the fear of inadequacy, but has not become less haunting for that. Consumer markets are eager to capitalize on that fear, and companies turning out consumer goods vie for the status of the most reliable guides and helpers in their clients' unending efforts to rise to the challenge. They supply 'the tools', the instruments required for the individually performed 'self-fabrication' job. The goods they present as 'tools' for individual use in decision-making are in fact decisions made in advance. They were ready-made well before the individual was confronted with the duty (presented as an opportunity) to decide. It is absurd to think of those tools as enabling individual choice of purpose. These instruments are the crystallizations of an irresistible 'necessity' – which, now as before, humans must learn, obey and learn to obey in order to be free . . .

Is not Facebook's mind-boggling success due to its role as a marketplace in which, every day, that stark necessity can meet with exhilarating freedom of choice?

DL You made the point a little earlier that Britain lags behind a country like South Korea in the extent to which social relationships among young people are electronically mediated. It is true, of course, that the market penetration – as they call it – of mobile media and of

Cyworld (the Korean equivalent of Facebook) is greater in South Korea than in the United Kingdom, but is there any reason why the UK will not catch up? I cannot think of one. However, 'catching up' may not be the best way to frame this because we're actually talking about rather different phenomena. Cyworld and Facebook are not the same. The dynamics differ with history and culture.

But in either case there are difficult questions. Sociology is now obliged to come to terms with the digital, or miss investigating and theorizing whole swathes of significant cultural activity. To begin with, the simple fact of technological dependence has to be factored into any social explanation worth its salt. So many relationships are conducted in part – or completely – online that a sociology without Facebook and its ilk is simply inadequate. Whatever an older generation makes of it, Facebook has quickly become a basic means of communicating – of 'connecting', as Facebook itself rightly calls it – and is now a dimension of daily life for millions.

Daniel Miller, for example, has a recent book, *Tales from Facebook* (2011), in which he shows how the digital medium is dovetailed with social life in quite profound ways. Couples can watch Facebook to discover if their 'relationship status' remains intact or has been changed by the other's mouse-click. In Miller's tales, these partners may blame Facebook for playing a role in a break-up, even while they continue to use it themselves. Even at this level, there are low-grade surveillant aspects, as partners also keep an eye on the competition and make their moves on the basis of what appears to be reliable intelligence on the screen.

So sociology has to deal with the digital. But it is one thing to note that electronic mediation is a rapidly rising phenomenon, and even to observe how, at work and play, in relationships at many levels and degrees of intensity, these new media must be 'factored in'. It is another to get to grips critically with the inner meanings of such mediation and to offer critical perspectives. Plainly, you don't attempt to hide your own concern about the apparently ephemeral and fragmentary relationships that seem to be fostered – or at least facilitated – by the new media.

Of course, you're not alone there. Sherry Turkle, who in the 1980s wrote approvingly of the experimental possibilities of new electronic media, for their role in developing what she called *The Second Self*, and pursued this in a fascinating way in *Life on the Screen* in the mid-1990s, has now changed her tone in *Alone Together*. As she says, 'These days, insecure in our relationships and anxious about intimacy, we look to technology for ways to be in relationships and to protect us from them at the same time.'[29] Her catchphrase is that we expect more from technology and less from each other.

I agree with you that sociology is ineluctably critical and also that it has to analyse what's actually happening. Sherry Turkle's work has taken a much more critical turn than it once evinced. But these queries about what sociologists might dub digital relationality take another twist when we think about the surveillant dimensions of new media. Not that pre-digital relationships were somehow exempt from surveillance – far from it – but rather that now particular kinds of surveillance are routinely involved in the digital mediation of relationships. This is true at several levels, from the everyday stalking (now usually referred to without disapproval) on social media to layers of marketing and other administrative surveillance online, that also affect relationships.[30]

So my question has to do with whether or to what extent digitally mediated relationships will always somehow be compromised by that technical fact or whether the digital can also support the social? It touches my own work on surveillance quite deeply because I have always maintained that one key problem with contemporary surveillance is its myopic focus on control, which quickly excludes any concern with *care*. As electronic technologies serve all too often to amplify some of the most questionable aspects of bureaucratic surveillance (more distancing, less focus on the face, which we'll discuss in a later conversation) should we conclude that *all* new surveillance is erosive of the social? Or, alternatively (and also to be discussed more later), are responsible and even *caring* forms of digital surveillance possible?

ZB You are absolutely right to pose these questions. Our life (and to a growing degree as we move from older to younger generations) is split between two universes, 'online' and 'offline', and irreparably bicentred. With our lives spanning two universes, each with substantive content and procedural rules of its own, we tend to deploy the same linguistic material when we move to and fro, without noticing the change of its semantic field at each crossing of the boundary. There is therefore no avoiding interpenetration; experience obtained in one universe cannot but re-form the axiology guiding the assessment of the other. Part of life spent in one of the two universes cannot be described correctly, its meaning cannot be grasped nor its logic and dynamics understood, without reference to the share played in its constitution by the second universe. Virtually every notion related to present-day life processes inevitably bears a mark of their bipolarity.

Josh Rose, whom I mentioned before, continued as if spurred by your (and, I would add, my) concerns

> I recently asked the question to my Facebook friends: 'Twitter, Facebook, Foursquare . . . is all this making you feel closer to people or farther away?' It sparked a lot of responses and seemed to touch one of our generation's exposed nerves. What is the effect of the Internet and social media on our humanity? From the outside view, digital interactions appear to be cold and inhuman. There's no denying that. And without doubt, given the choice between hugging someone and 'poking' someone, I think we can all agree which one feels better. The theme of the responses to my Facebook question seemed to be summed up by my friend Jason, who wrote: 'Closer to people I'm far away from'. Then, a minute later, wrote, 'but maybe farther from the people I'm close enough to'. And then added, 'I just got confused.' It *is* confusing. We live in this paradox now, where two seemingly conflicting realities exist side-by-side. Social media simultaneously draws us nearer and distances us.

Admittedly, Rose was wary of passing unambiguous verdicts – as indeed one should be in the case of such a seminal yet hazardous transaction as the exchange of sparse incidents of offline 'closeness' for the massive online variety. The 'closeness' traded away was perhaps more satisfying, yet time and energy consuming and beset with risks; the 'closeness' traded into is no doubt faster, calls for almost no effort and is almost risk-free, but many find it much less able to quash the thirst for fully fledged company. You gain something, you lose something else – and it is awfully difficult to decide whether your gains compensate for the losses; besides, a once-and-for-all decision is out of the question – you will find the option as brittle and until-further-notice as the 'closeness' you've acquired.

What you've acquired is a network, not a 'community'. As you'll find sooner or later (provided, of course, that you haven't forgotten or failed to learn what a 'community' was all about, busy as you are in piecing networks together and pulling them apart), they are no more similar than chalk and cheese. Belonging to a community is a much more secure and reliable condition than having a network – though admittedly with more constraints and obligations. Community watches you closely and leaves you little room for manoeuvre (it may ban you and exile you, but it won't allow you to opt out of your own will). But a network may care little, or not at all, about your obedience to its norms (if a network has norms to obey, that is, which all too often it doesn't) and so it gives you much more rope, and above all will not penalize you for quitting. You can count on a community to be a 'friend in need, and so a friend indeed'. But networks are there mostly to share the fun, and their readiness to come to your rescue in the event of trouble unrelated to that shared 'focus of interest' is hardly ever put to the test, and if it were it would pass it even less frequently. All in all, the choice is between security and freedom: you need both, but you cannot have one without sacrificing a part at least of the other; and the more you have of one, the less you'll have of the other. For security, the old-style communities beat networks hands down. For freedom, it is the other way round (after all, it takes only one press of the 'delete' key or a decision to stop answering messages to get free of its interference).

Besides, there is all that enormous, indeed deep and unfathomable difference between 'hugging' and 'poking' someone, as Rose puts it . . . In other words, between the online variety of 'closeness' and its offline prototype: between depth and shallowness, profundity and superficiality, warmth and coolness, the heartfelt and the perfunctory. You choose, and in all probability you will go on choosing and you can hardly avoid choosing, but it is better to choose knowing what you are choosing – and be prepared to pay the price of your choice. This is at least what Rose seems to imply, and there is no quarrelling with his advice. Just as Sherry Turkle realizes, in the passage you quote: 'These days, insecure in our relationships and anxious about intimacy, we look to technology for ways to be in relationships and to protect us from them at the same time.'

So are the names and the photos that Facebook users call 'friends' close or distant? A dedicated 'active user' of Facebook boasted recently that he managed to make 500 new friends in a day – that is, more than I've managed in all my 86 years of a long life. But as Professor Robin Dunbar, evolutionary anthropologist at Oxford, insists, 'our minds are not designed [by evolution] to allow us to have more than a very limited number of people in our social world'. Dunbar actually calculated that number: he found that 'most of us can maintain only around 150 meaningful relationships'. Not unexpectedly, he's called that limit imposed by (biological) evolution the 'Dunbar number'. This is, we may comment, the point to which biological evolution brought our remote ancestors and where it stopped, or at least slowed down sharply, leaving the field to its much nimbler, more agile and dextrous, and above all more resourceful and less patient successor – called 'cultural evolution' (that is, evolution triggered, shaped and driven by humans themselves, through the teaching and learning process rather than the changing arrangement of genes).

Let me note that 150 was probably the topmost number of creatures who could come together, stay together and profitably cooperate while surviving only on hunting and gathering; the size of a proto-human herd couldn't manage to cross that magic border without summoning, or rather conjuring up, forces and (yes!) tools beyond fangs and talons. Without those other forces and tools, called 'cultural', the continuous proximity of larger numbers would have been unsustainable, and so the capacity to 'hold in the mind' those larger numbers would have been superfluous. 'Imagining' totalities larger than those accessible to the senses was as uncalled for as it was inconceivable. Minds had no need to store what senses had no opportunity to grasp. . . was the arrival of culture bound to coincide, as it did, with trespassing over the 'Dunbar number'? Was passing over that number the first act of transgression of 'natural limits' – and given that the transgression of limits (whether 'natural' or self-set) is culture's defining trait and its mode of being, was this also the birth act of culture?[31]

The electronically sustained 'networks of friendship' promised to break through the recalcitrant limitations to sociability set by our genetically transmitted equipment. Well, says Dunbar, they didn't and won't – the promise is destined to be broken. 'Yes,' says Dunbar in his opinion piece of 25 December 2010 in the *New York Times*, 'you can "friend" 500, 1,000, even 5,000 people with your Facebook page, but all save the core 150 are mere voyeurs looking into your daily life.' Among those thousands of Facebook friends, 'meaningful relationships', whether serviced electronically or lived offline, are confined as before inside the impassable limits of the 'Dunbar number'. The true service rendered by Facebook and its ilk, the 'social' websites, is the maintenance of a steady core of friends in the context of a highly mobile, fast-moving and fast-changing world . . .

Our distant ancestors had it easy: they, like their nearest and dearest, tended on the whole to dwell in the same place from cradle to coffin, in close proximity to each other and within reach and sight of each other. This kind of, we might say, 'topographic' foundation of long-term, even lifelong bonds is unlikely to appear now, and even less likely to be immune to the flow of time, vulnerable as it is to the vicissitudes of individual life histories. Fortunately, we now have ways of 'staying in touch' that are fully and truly 'extraterritorial' and so independent of the degree and frequency of physical proximity. 'Facebook and other social networking sites', and only they – so Dunbar suggests – 'allow us to keep up the friendships that would otherwise rapidly wither away'. This is not, though, the end of the benefits they offer: 'they allow us to reintegrate our networks so that, rather than having several disconnected subsets of friends, we can rebuild, *albeit virtually*, the kind of old rural communities where everyone knew everyone else' (emphasis added). In the case of friendship at any rate, Dunbar implies, even if not in so many words, that Marshall McLuhan's idea of the 'media being the message' has been refuted; though his other memorable suggestion, that of the arrival of a 'global village', came true for a change. Albeit virtually . . .

There are reasons to suspect that it was precisely those facilities that secured and assured for the 'social networking' sites their tremendous popularity, making their chief marketer, Mark Elliot Zuckerberg, an instant multibillionaire. It was those facilities that allowed the modern drive for effortlessness, convenience and comfort to finally reach, conquer and colonize the hitherto stubbornly and passionately independent land of human bonds. They made that land risk-free, or almost, making any overstaying of their welcome by ex-desirables impossible, or almost. They made cutting one's losses cost-free, or almost. All in all, they accomplished the feat of squaring the circle, of eating the cake and having it: by cleansing the business of interrelating from any strings attached, they removed the ugly fly of unbreakability that used to blight the sweet ointment of human togetherness.

DL Much of what you say resonates with me, Zygmunt. But for my part, I'm acutely aware of the fact that I'm not part of the Facebook generation. I'm what they call a digital immigrant who has had to learn his way in a new culture, not a digital native, for whom Facebook is a taken-for-granted and indispensable way of connecting with others. Of course, we can see the ways that Facebook users are commodified; that 'friend' as we understand the term is an incongruous word to use of a thousand people; and that as a tool of surveillance, Facebook not only draws usable data from people, it also, brilliantly, permits them to do the initial classifications by identifying themselves as 'friends'. Talk about collusion with surveillance! But it's all too easy to see how people might be *used* by Facebook and forget that, equally, people *use* Facebook, constantly, enthusiastically, addictively.

In surveillance studies it's all too easy for us to end up treating Facebook users (or anyone else for that matter) as cultural dupes. We may acknowledge that social media aficionados find connective benefits in their posts, messages, photos, updates, likes and pokes, but simultaneously give the impression that the ways they are tracked and trapped by their data trails completely outweigh the significance of their enjoyment. So I'm wondering if you would comment on a couple of questions that seem pertinent to me in this regard?

The first is this: How do you explain the palpable popularity of social media? Could it be that in a liquid modern world of short-term relationships, commitments 'until further notice' and high levels of mobility and speed, social media fill (however inadequately) a gap? Old face-to-face communities of the village where everyone knows everyone else are the stuff of romanticized historical novels or, for some, claustrophobic memory. But the desire to find friends, however friable, or at least to make some human connections, is still strong and perhaps even prompted by some felt losses of 'community'.

The second follows: If social media are actively *used by* people for their own purposes, then what happens when those purposes are opposed to the corporations or governments who might be thought of as *using* them? Consider these examples: A McDonald's Twitter campaign, using a hashtag to generate supportive stories about good dining experiences, backfired when disgruntled customers used the opportunity to complain about food poisoning and poor service.[32] If Facebook and its users have conflicts, they're almost always over how personal information is used. Several new features, such as Beacon or Timeline, have ignited the ire of users challenging Facebook's firefighting, skill at dousing the flames. And on another plane, social media have been prominently deployed in a number of protests and democracy movements from the so-called Arab Spring to the Occupy events of 2011. Sure, this also enabled authorities to keep track of protesters, but does that annul social media's usefulness for social organizing?

This is a complex question, I know, and you have already pointed out that social media excel in creating *networks*. These are characterized by weak ties, which are good at increasing participation or sparking new ideas and information – embarrassing McDonald's, for instance. But are they perhaps different from the kinds of relationships with strong ties that tend to foster persistence, self-sacrifice and risk-taking?[33] Yet even as I say that, it does seem that some of these features of commitments with strong ties are visible at least in some Arab Spring countries.

ZB What you are saying is that a knife can be used to slice bread and cut throats . . . no doubt you are right. But different breads and throats are cut in the case of that particular knife called online connections/disconnections, integration/separations, and what I mostly talk about is the stuff of interpersonal interaction and interpersonal bonds to which that particular knife is applied; especially in their – sort of – 'media is the message' effect.

Let me briefly illustrate that ambiguity by the case of online mediated and operated sex. And let me refer for this purpose to the observation of the brilliant and thorough Jean-Claude Kaufmann that thanks to the 'computerization' of dating and 'getting together' sex is 'now more confused than ever'. Jean-Claude Kaufmann hit the bull's eye in those words. He says:

> According to the romantic ideal, it all began with senti-ment, which then developed into desire. Love led (via marriage) to sex. We now seem to have two very different options: we can either cheerfully indulge in sex as a leisure activity, or we can opt for a long-term commitment. The first option means that self-control is primarily a ques-tion of avoiding commitment: we are careful not to fall (too much) in love . . . The dividing line between sex and sentiment is becoming increasingly ill-defined.[34]

Kaufmann sets out to lay bare that entanglement, though not to disentangle what has been shown to be as resistant to every and any disentangling effort as the Gordian knot was considered to be . . .

The two options, Kaufmann points out, correspond to two conflicting models of 'individuality': accord-ingly, contemporary individuals pressed to follow both are likely to be pulled in two opposite directions. On one hand, there is the 'economic model, which assumes that individuals always act on the basis of rational self-interest . . . The alternative model is supplied by love . . . This model allows the individual to abandon the egotis-tical self of old and to devote him- or herself to others.' (This description of love, though, is not in my view quite correct: the 'economic' and the 'love' models certainly stand in sharp opposition to each other – but not in the way selfishness and altruism do; it is rather that the 'economic model' casts egoism and altruism – 'being good to oneself' and 'being good to others' – as conflicting attitudes; while in love the two apparent opposites and sworn enemies mingle, coalesce and blend – and are no longer separable or distinguishable from each other.)

The first option is construed after the 'consumerist illusion':

> it would have us believe that we can choose a man (or a woman) in the same way that we choose a yoghurt in the hypermarket. But that is not how love works. Love is not reducible to consumerism, and that is probably a good thing. The difference between a man and a yoghurt is that a woman cannot introduce a man into her life and expect everything to remain the same.

But, courtesy of the 'consumerist illusion',

> it all feels so safe. She can log on with one click, and log off with another click . . . An individual armed with a mouse imagines that she is in complete and absolute control of her social contacts . . . All the usual obstacles appear to have vanished, and a world of endless possibilities opens up . . . A woman on the net is like a child who has been let loose in a sweetshop.

All looks neat, safe and nice, unless . . . Yes, here is the snag: unless sentiments arise and love worms itself in, befuddling the judgement.

In places, Kaufmann comes dangerously close to laying the responsibility for such confusion on the deceitful meekness and docility of the computer mouse and the computer revolution that thrust it in everybody's hands; but he is aware that the roots of the problem reach much deeper into the existential dilemmas into which present-day society casts its members. He makes the right point in the end: 'Society is obsessed with the search for pleasure, has a taste for adventure and is interested in new and more intense sensations, but it also needs the stability and reassurance that encourage us to avoid risk-taking and not to go too far. That is why current developments appear to be so contradictory.' Well, not just appear, let me comment. They *are* contradictory. As contradictory as the need for freedom and the need for adventure, and as the socially provided tools and stratagems serving each of those needs but hardly ever both of them simultaneously.

We are all in a double-bind – a tangle with no clear and risk-free exit. If you opt for security first, you need to give up many of the dream-like experiences which new sexual freedoms go on promising to deliver, and often do. If you are after freedom first, however, forget about a partner you may need to hold your hand when you are stumbling through a landscape full of treacherous bogs and quicksand. Between the two resolutions, a wide open, overflowing Pandora's box! The curse of internet dating comes from the same source to which we tend to trace its blessing, so Kaufmann rightly suggests. It emanates from an 'intermediary zone in which nothing is really preordained [and] no one knows in advance what is going to happen'. In other words, from a space in which anything might happen yet nothing can be done with any measure of certainty, trust and self-assurance, however small.

Computers are not the culprits, contrary to what some of their 'surfing' rather than diving and fathoming critics imply: computers owe the lightning speed of their brilliant career to offering their users a better opportunity to do what they always wished to do yet could not for lack of suitable tools. But neither are they the saviours, as their genuflecting enthusiasts are only too eager to aver. This mess is rooted in the way our existential predicament is tackled and deployed by the kind of society we have constructed while being constructed by it. And to extricate ourselves from that mess (if it is conceivable at all) would need more than changing the tools – which, after all, only assist us in doing what we would be trying to do anyway, whether in a cottage-industry fashion or using cutting-edge technology that is all the rage.

The phenomenon of twitters and blogs summoning people to the streets and public squares is another illustration of the same ambiguity. What was first rehearsed verbally on Facebook and Twitter is now being experienced in the flesh. And without losing the traits that made it so endearing when it was practised on the web: the ability to enjoy the present without mortgaging the future, rights without obligations.

The breathtakingly intoxicating experience of togetherness; perhaps, who knows, too early to say, solidarity. That change, already occurring, means: no longer alone. And it has taken so little effort to accomplish – little more than pushing in a 'd' in the place of the 't' in that nasty word 'solitary'. Solidarity on demand, and as long lasting as the demand endures (and not a minute longer). Solidarity not so much in sharing the chosen cause as solidarity in having a cause; I and you and all the rest of us ('us', that is, the people on the square) having a purpose, and life having a meaning.

A few months ago young people in a vigil in tents pitched around Wall Street sent a letter of invitation to Lech Wałęsa, the legendary leader of the equally legendary Polish Solidarity movement, famous for setting in motion the dismantling of the Soviet empire through shipyard workers, miners and factory workers stubbornly staying inside their dockyards, mines or factories until their demands were met. In that letter, the young people gathered on Manhattan's streets and squares underlined that they were students and trade union members of many races and with the most variegated life stories and political ideas, united solely by their wish to 'restore its moral purity to the American economy'; that they had no leader except the shared belief that 99 per cent of Americans wouldn't and couldn't tolerate any longer the greed and rapacity of the 1 per cent. The authors of the letter said that Solidarity in Poland set an example of how walls and barriers could be demolished and the impossible be made possible; an example they intended to follow.

The same or quite similar words could be written by the throngs of young and not so young people of the 15th May *movimiento los indignados* billowing through the city squares of Madrid and its counterparts in 951 cities of more than 90 countries. None of those movements has a leader; they draw their enthusiastic supporters from all walks of life, races, religions and political camps, united solely by their refusal to allow things to go on as they are. Each of them has a single barrier or wall in mind, earmarked to be shattered and destroyed. These barriers may vary from one country to another, but each is believed to block the way to a better kind of society, a kind more hospitable to humanity and less tolerant of inhumanity. Each selected barrier is viewed as the one whose dismantling is bound to put an end to every and any instance of the suffering that brought the protesters together: as the link it is necessary to topple to set the whole chain in motion. Asking about the shape of things thereafter should happen only once that has been done and the building site for the new and improved society has been cleared. As the English used to say, 'we'll cross that bridge when we come to it'.

In this combination of focusing on a single task of demolition while leaving vague the image of the world the day after the demolition lies the strength of people in the streets – as well as their weakness. We already have ample proof that movements of the indignant are indeed all-powerful in acting as demolition squads; however, proof of their capacities as designing and building teams is still outstanding. A few months ago we all watched with bated breath and rising admiration the wondrous spectacle of the Arab Spring. It is late October when I write these words – but we are still waiting, so far in vain, for the Arab Summer . . .

And Wall Street took little note of 'being occupied' by the offline visitors from the online world.

2

Liquid surveillance as post-panoptic

David Lyon Among those who are new to the serious study of surveillance, the idea of the panopticon seems like a brilliant idea. It is on one level a theory of how surveillance works and on another a means of situating surveillance within the story of modernity. For Foucault, who famously lighted on Bentham's panopticon design as offering a key to understanding the rise of modern, self-disciplining societies, the panopticon is pivotal.

However, for some who have studied surveillance for some time, mere mention of the panopticon elicits exasperated groans. For them, too much has been expected by too many of the panopticon with the result that the diagram is wheeled out at every conceivable opportunity to, well, explain surveillance. So we come across electronic panopticons and superpanopticons as well as variations such as the synopticon or the polyopticon. Enough! advises Kevin Haggerty, let's 'tear down the walls'![35] There are historical as well as logical limits to the usefulness of panoptic imagery today.

Yet, without doubt, Foucault made some fascinating and important observations about the panopticon, showing how it truly is a mirror of modernity in some significant respects. He saw discipline as key; controlling the 'soul' to change behaviour and motivation. There is something searching, and compelling, about his statement: 'He who is subjected to a field of visibility, and who knows it, assumes responsibility for the constraints of power; he makes them play spontaneously upon himself; he inscribes in himself the power relation in which he simultaneously plays both roles; he becomes the principle of his own subjection.'[36] This is how, as Foucault also says, visibility becomes a trap, but it is a trap that we ourselves help to construct. If one were to apply the panoptic diagram to thinking about surveillance today, that insight alone would be worth exploring. How do we inscribe surveillance power in ourselves when we go online, use a credit card, show our passports or apply for government assistance?

It is also true that Foucault helped us see how power relations characterize all manner of social situations, not merely one in which attempts to control or to manage a population – as with the police or border officials – are more overt and obvious. Thus one might not be surprised to find, for example, consumer surveillance through database marketing described as 'panoptic', as Oscar Gandy did, classically, in his work on *The Panoptic Sort: A Political Economy of Personal Information*.[37] Here, of course, the relation to the original panoptic principle may become a little strained (we'll come back to this).

But the attempt to use the panopticon today can

also produce apparently paradoxical outcomes. Lorna Rhodes's exploration of the 'supermax' – maximum security – prison, for example, leads her to conclude that the panopticon may 'diagnose us all'.[38] She shows how the supermax experience prompts some inmates to self-mutilate; the panoptic 'calculated manipulation' of the body calls forth its opposite. Experiencing their bodies as abandoned, these inmates use their bodies to assert themselves. They react against the negative visibility intended to produce compliance with acts aimed at heightened visibility.[39]

On the other hand, in the work of Oscar Gandy, and more recently in that of Mark Andrejevic,[40] the panoptic triage is seen operating in a consumer context. This is the soft end of the surveillance continuum. In database marketing the idea is to lull intended targets into thinking that they count when all it wants is to count them and, of course, to suck them into further purchases. Here, the individuation is clearly commodified; if it is panoptic power, it is in the service of marketers, intent on lulling and luring the unwary. But the findings of Gandy and Andrejevic suggest that such techniques work, routinely. They feature within a thriving and lucrative marketing industry.

So here is the paradox: the sharp end of the panoptic spectrum may generate moments of refusal and resistance that militate against the production of Foucault's 'docile bodies', whereas the soft end seems to seduce participants into a stunning conformity of which some seem scarcely conscious.[41] Paradoxes like this do raise vital questions of the body and of technologies, of productive power and active resistance, and of the hiddenness or mutuality of vision, to name but three.

But they also insert nagging doubts about how fruitful panoptic analysis can be today.

Which is why I want to ask you about the panopticon, Zygmunt. After all, you were writing cogently about this theme long before I was and you have used the critique of the panopticon many times as a means of indicating how contemporary modernities have gone beyond some of their earlier features. Indeed, you use the panopticon as part of the 'before' story of which the 'after' is now liquid modernity. The world of fixity dissolved into flows; the dispersal of disciplines into new spaces, new situations.

I shall start with this direct and general question before we try to tease out some of the particulars: Does the advent of liquid surveillance mean forgetting the panopticon?

Zygmunt Bauman Myself, I would not share Kevin Haggerty's concerns . . . Already quite a few decades ago I was inoculated against this and similar alarms, having been forewarned by the great psychologist Gordon Allport that we in the humanities never solve any issues – we only get bored with them. And calls to forget have since turned into the most common as well as the most treacherous siren songs pouring from the loudspeakers or earpieces of the liquid modern era . . .

As I see it, the panopticon is alive and well, armed in fact with (electronically enhanced, 'cyborgized') muscles so mighty that Bentham or even Foucault could not and would not have imagined them – but it has clearly stopped being the universal pattern or strategy of domination that both those authors believed it was in their times; it is no longer even the principal or most commonly practised pattern or strategy. The panopticon has been shifted and confined to the 'unmanageable' parts of society, such as prisons, camps, psychiatric clinics and other 'total institutions', in Erving Goffman's sense. How they work nowadays has been superbly recorded and in my view definitively described by Loïc Wacquant. In other words, panopticon-like practices are limited to sites for humans booked to the debit side, declared useless and fully and truly 'excluded' – and where the incapacitation of bodies, rather than their harnessing to useful work, is the sole purpose behind the setting's logic.

In view of that, Lorna Rhodes's finding does not appear that 'paradoxical' after all. The cooperation of the ruled was always welcomed by rulers and an integral part of their calculation. Self-immolation and self-inflicted damage to bodies, all the way to self-destruction, is all but the explicit or implicit objective of panoptical techniques when they are applied to the useless and altogether unprofitable elements. Most certainly, such cooperation on the part of victims would not be seriously frowned upon, deprecated and regretted, whatever noises might be made to the contrary! The genius of ruling wants the ruled to do the rulers' job – and the inmates of supermax prisons hasten to oblige. The 'totality' of that kind of total institution manifests itself precisely in that the only way of 'self-asserting' open to the ruled is to do with their own hands what the rulers dearly wish to attain. The precedents, if you need any, were the prisoners who threw themselves on the high-voltage barbed wire in Auschwitz. Though no one suggested then or afterwards that thereby the 'calculated manipulation' resulted in its opposite!

I do not know for sure whether Étienne de la Boétie did exist, or whether Michel de Montaigne invented him to offload the threat of being penalized for composing a highly risky, debunking and rebellious text (the jury in this case is still out) – but whoever its author was, the *Discourse of Voluntary Servitude* is still worth rereading, particularly by those who are dazzled by novelties and fail to spot continuity behind discontinuities.

Whoever the author was, he or she presaged the stratagem developed several centuries later to near perfection in the liquid modern society of consumers. Everything – pattern of domination, philosophy and pragmatic precepts of management, vehicles of social control, the very concept of power (that is, of the way to manipulate probabilities to increase the likelihood of desirable conduct and reduce to a minimum the chances of the opposite) – seems to be moving in the same direction. Everything moves from enforcement to temptation and seduction, from normative regulation to PR, from policing to the arousal of desire; and everything shifts the principal role in achieving the intended and welcome results from the bosses to the subordinates, from supervisors to the supervised, from surveyors to the surveyed; in short, from the managers to the managed.

And there is another trend closely intertwined with the first, one that is sometimes summed up in an unduly impoverishing dilemma of stick and carrot. But it manifests itself in many and different seminal shifts, and above all in the translocation of the wager in every and any struggle for success from discipline, obedience, conformity, order-following, routine, uniformity and a reduction of options – all in all from the predetermination of subordinates' choices by means addressed to their rational faculty of reward seeking and penalty avoidance – to essentially 'irrational' faculties of initiative, adventurousness, experimentation, self-assertion, emotionality and pleasure and entertainment seeking. If Bentham saw the key to managerial success in reducing the choices of the panopticon's inmates to the bare-bone alternatives of a dull job or an even deadlier boredom, a daily bowl of gruel or the torments of hunger, contemporary managers worth their salt would see in the recommended regime an abominable as well as unforgivably inane waste of the capital resources hidden in personal idiosyncrasies and growing in line with their variety and variegation. It is now the counting on human rationality alone, coupled with the suppression of wayward emotions, that leading managers, attuned as they are to the spirit of the time, would dismiss as inexcusably irrational . . .

Having considered bureaucracy as the fullest incarnation of modern rationality, Max Weber proceeded to enumerate the features which any purposeful arrangement of human activities needs to acquire and strive to perfect, in addition to strict hierarchies of command and reporting, in order to come close to bureaucracy's ideal type and so climb to the peak of rationality. At the top of Weber's list was the exclusion of all personal loyalties, commitments, beliefs and preferences other than those declared relevant to serving the purpose of the organization; everything 'personal', that is not determined by the statute books of the company, needed to be left in the cloakroom at the entry to the building, so to speak, and collected back after the completion of 'office time'. Today, when the centre of gravity, burden of proof and responsibility for the result has been dropped by managers, as team leaders and unit commanders, on to the shoulders of individual performers, or 'contracted out', 'outsourced' or 'hived off' laterally and judged according to a seller–buyer pattern rather than a boss–subordinate relationship, the aim is to harness the totality of the subaltern personality and their whole waking time to the company's purposes. This is an expedient viewed, not without reason, as infinitely more convenient and profitable than the notoriously costly, unwieldy, restrictive and unduly laborious panoptical measures. Servitude, along with surveillance of performance twenty-four hours a day and seven days a week, is becoming fully and truly a DIY job for the subordinates. The construction, running and servicing of panopticons have been turned from a liability into an asset for the bosses, written into the small print of every contract of employment.

In a nutshell, just as snails carry their homes, so the employees of the brave new liquid modern world must grow and carry their personal panopticons on their own bodies. Employees and every other variety of the subordinated have been charged with full and unconditional responsibility for keeping them in good repair and assuring their uninterrupted operation (leaving your mobile or iPhone at home when you go for a stroll, and thereby suspending the state of being constantly at a superior's beck and call, is a case of serious misdemeanour). Tempted by the allure of consumer markets and frightened by the new freedom of the bosses to vanish, together with the jobs on offer, subordinates are so groomed to the role of self-watchers as to render redundant the watchtowers in the Bentham/Foucault scheme.

DL I hear you saying, Zygmunt, that the classic pan-opticon is a thing of the past for the vast majority in the global north, except in so far as this majority have to carry their 'personal panopticons' with them. The classic panopticon is really only visible at the margins, particularly in urban areas where the poor, as Wacquant says, are 'outcasts'. And I agree wholeheartedly with you that acute forms of something suspiciously like the panopticon still lurk in such places. Wacquant's 'social panopticism' is found in the guise of programmes to promote the well-being of deprived households but which actually submit them to 'an ever more precise and penetrating form of punitive surveillance'.[42] This kind of motif is also very visible in John Gilliom's book *Overseers of the Poor*, in which he examines how women on welfare are subjected to the use of highly invasive computer-assisted casework (but who, intriguingly but unsurprisingly, find many ways to subvert the system for the sake of their children).[43]

So let's follow this thread through a little more before I ask you to reflect on one or two of the other contemporary variations on panopticon analysis that nudge us to allow a broader analysis some room. You suggest that the panopticon may still be found at the margins, in total institutions and the like. Wacquant's work focuses on a social panopticism in run-down and deprived areas of cities, in the global south as well as the global north. But do you think that the same kind of analysis might be applied to marginal groups as such, would-be immigrants, suspected 'terrorists' and others subject to more recent 'security' regimes? Didier Bigo's variation on the panoptic theme speaks of the 'ban-opticon' and applies to just such global marginals.

Simply put, Bigo proposes 'ban-opticon' to indicate how profiling technologies are used to determine who is placed under specific surveillance. But it emerges from a full theoretical analysis of how a new 'globalized (in)security' emerges from the increasingly concerted activities of international 'managers of unease' such as police, border officials and airline companies. Transnational bureaucracies of surveillance and control, both businesses and politicians, now work at a distance to monitor and control population movement, through surveillance. Taken together, these discourses, practices, physical architectures and rules form a complete, connected apparatus, or what Foucault called *dispositif*. The outcome is not a global panopticon but a 'ban-opticon' – combining Jean-Luc Nancy's idea of the 'ban' as developed by Agamben, with Foucault's 'opticon'. Its *dispositif* shows who is welcome or not, creating categories of people excluded not just from a given nation-state but from a rather amorphous and not unified cluster of global powers. And it operates virtually, using networked databases to channel flows of data, especially data about what is yet to happen, as in the film and book of *Minority Report*.

Rather like you, Bigo insists that there is no centralized manifestation of the panopticon today, and if the *dispositif* exists at all it is fragmented and heterogeneous. It operates through state and corporate entities, which along with other agencies 'converge towards the strengthening of the informatic and biometrics as modes of surveillance that focus on the trans-border movements of individuals'.[44] This is, says Bigo, a form of insecurity at the transnational level (and not a panopticon at all). Within it, Bigo analyses discourses (risk and threat levels, enemies within and so on), institutions, architectural structures (from detention centres to airport passenger flow lanes), laws and administrative measures – each of which singles out certain groups for special treatment. The strategic function of the ban-opticon diagram is to profile a minority as 'unwelcome'. Its three features are exceptional power within liberal societies (states of emergency that become routine), profiling (excluding some groups, categories of proactively excluded people, because of their potential future behaviour) and the normalizing of non-excluded groups (to a belief in the free movement of goods, capital, information and persóns). The ban-opticon operates in globalized spaces beyond the nation-state, so the effects of power and resistance are no longer felt merely between state and society.

Bigo sees that at this point – the division into what you call 'globals and locals' – his work and yours converge. Yet he also wonders if you underestimate the ways in which 'globals' are normalized into the 'imperative of mobility' through some of the mutually dependent strategies of the same *dispositif*. The discourses on free movement normalize the majority. It's still not a full-blown or even a shadow panopticon, of course, but it helps to explain why your 'globals' practise their peripatetic lifestyles as they do *and* (I would add) why they come to believe that the ban-opticon is necessary for others. (Perhaps these are the 'personal panopticons' that you say the majority carry as their snail shells?) Bigo speaks of all this hinging on the activities of those he calls the 'managers of unease' – security professionals and others – who are closest to the *dispositif* that controls and surveils certain groups beyond the majority.

So my question is this: How far do you think these kinds of variations on the panopticon theme, which still recognize the significance of the Foucauldian *dispositif* but go beyond it to address present-day political economies and technologies in globalizing contexts, help us grasp what's happening in liquid modern times? In this case, the analysis seems close to what you want to pursue (and that you discussed, for instance, in *Globalization*) – or not?

ZB Bigo focuses on unwanted migrants, but surveillance technology installed at state borderposts is just one case of a 'ban-opticon' (by the way, I find 'ban-opticon' a felicitous term, even if it is more redolent of a word-play than of semantic logic). It is just one case, that is, of a more general phenomenon of surveillance philosophy and surveilling equipment wrapped around the task of 'keeping away' instead of 'keeping in', as the panopticon did, and drawing its life juices and developmental energy from the currently unstoppable rise of *securitarian* preoccupations, not from the *disciplining* urge as in the case of the panopticon. I suggest that CCTV cameras surrounding gated communities and dotting shopping malls and the forecourts of supermarkets are the principal – the most common and pattern-setting – specimens of ban-optical devices. The ban-opticon guards the entrances to the parts of the world inside which DIY surveillance suffices to maintain and reproduce 'order'; primarily, it bars entry to all those who possess none of the tools of DIY surveillance (of the credit card or Blackberry kind) and who therefore cannot be relied on to practise such surveillance on their own. These individuals (more to the point, *categories* of individuals) must be 'power assisted', so to speak, in falling into line with the behavioural patterns of 'defensible spaces'. Another task of ban-optical appliances, a task of no less gravity, is to promptly spot individuals who show signs of an unwillingness to fall into line or who plot to breach those binding patterns.

In other words, surveillance technology today develops on two fronts, serving two opposite strategic objectives: confinement (or 'fencing in') on one front line, exclusion (or 'fencing out') on the other. The surge in the global mass of exiles, refugees, asylum-seekers – or seekers of bread and drinking water – may indeed boost *both* kinds of surveillance technology (I suppose that Bigo would agree). In his latest book, Michel Agier sums up his ten-year field study in the refugee camps scattered across Africa and South America, as well as in European 'detention centres' for immigrants defined as 'illegal' or suspended in the 'no laws, no rights' status of 'asylum-seekers'.[45] He concludes that seventy years later Benjamin's 'bad luck' (as Hannah Arendt dubbed his stopping at the French-Spanish border that led to his suicide) has all but lost its 'extraordinary' status, not to mention its apparent singularity. Already in 1950, 1 million refugees (mainly people 'displaced' by the war) had been counted in official global statistics. Today, the conservative estimate of the numbers of 'people in transition' is 12 million – but as many as 1 *billion* refugees-turned-exiles and ensconced in the nowhere-land of camps are predicted for 2050.

'Being in transition' is, of course, an ironic expression when it is applied to the lot of Walter Benjamin and the fast expanding mass of its mimeographed replicas. By definition, the idea of 'transition' stands for a finite process, a time-span with clearly drawn starting and finishing lines – a *passage* from a spatial, temporal, or spatial *and* temporal, 'here' to a 'there'; but these are precisely the attributes denied to the condition of 'being a refugee', which is defined and set apart from and in opposition to the 'norms' by their absence. A 'camp' is not a mid-station, or a road inn, or a motel on a voyage from here to there. It is the terminal station, where all mapped roads peter out and all movement grinds to a halt – with little prospect of parole or of the sentence being completed: more and more people are born in camps and die there, visiting no other places in their lifetime. Camps ooze finality; not the finality of destination, though, but of the state of transition petrified into a state of permanence.

The name 'transition camp', commonly selected by power-holders for the places where refugees are ordered to stay, is an oxymoron: 'transition' is the very quality whose denial and absence defines the status of a refugee. The sole defined meaning of being assigned to a place called a 'refugee camp' is that all other conceivable places are cast as off-limits. The sole meaning of being an insider in a refugee camp is to be an outsider, a stranger, an alien body, an intruder in the rest of the world – challenging that rest of the world to surround itself with ban-optical devices; in a nutshell, becoming an inmate of a refugee camp means eviction from the world shared by the rest of humanity. 'Having been evicted', being fixed in the *exile* condition, is all there is and needs to be in the identity of the refugee. And as Agier repeatedly points out, it is not the issue of *where from* one has come into the encampment, but the absence of a *where to* – the declared prohibition or practical impossibility of arriving anywhere else – that sets an exile apart from the rest of humanity. Being set apart is what counts.

Exiles don't need to cross state borders, to arrive from another country. They may be, and all too often are, born and bred inside the country where their life of exile is lived. They might not even have moved an inch from the place where they were born. Agier has every right to collapse refugee camps, encampments of the homeless and urban ghettoes into the same category – of the 'corridors of exile'. Legal or illegal residents of all such places share one decisive trait: they are all redundant. The rejects or refuse of society. To sum up, waste. 'Waste', by definition, is the antonym of 'utility'; it denotes objects without possible use. Indeed, the sole accomplishment of waste is soiling and cluttering up the space that could otherwise be usefully employed. The principal purpose of the ban-opticon is to make sure that the waste is separated from decent product and ear-marked for transportation to a refuse tip. Once it is on it, the panopticon will see to it that the waste stays there – preferably until biodegradation completes its course.

DL Thank you, Zygmunt. It's both instructive and stimulating to see how our work on surveillance dove-tails with – and sometimes differs from – yours. But before leaving this, can we take just one more crack at the panopticon theme? We've agreed, I think, that the ban-opticon is where the panopticon urge may now be seen most blatantly, and that this kind of analysis speaks to some depressingly common experiences in a globalizing world. But surveillance scholars have also wrestled with these ideas in at least two contexts that refer to majority populations rather than to contexts of minority 'waste'.

I'm thinking on the one hand of the compelling studies of consumer surveillance carried out by Oscar Gandy, originally under the title *The Panoptic Sort*. I referred to this earlier but now I'd like us to tease out this strand a bit more. Gandy's argument in that early book is that a general sorting machine is evident in the world of database marketing and so-called geodemographics. People get clustered into crude population segments so that marketers can treat them differently depending on their consumer behaviour. Although some Foucault scholars might dispute this, Gandy's use of the panopticon is both to examine how the panopticon 'works' today in consumer settings, *and*, crucially, to show how the logic of the panopticon affects those who find themselves within its gaze.

As I see it, Gandy combines the analysis of the sorting and classifying aspects of the panopticon with the process whereby consumers are processed.[46] However, while he obtains his ideas on the classifying aspect of the panopticon from Foucault, he is more explicit about his analysis also being a 'political economy of personal information'. Marketers are always seeking new ways to rationalize the market by singling out for special attention consumers whose attributes make them attractive 'targets of opportunity'.[47] Other potential consumers can be allowed to slip out of sight while the truly worthy ones are skimmed off. The sorting process here focuses on those who, so far from being marginalized, already benefit from the system. This is the 'bourgeois form of monitored mobility', according to Mark Andrejevic,[48] suited to the smartphone, SUV and cruise-line crowd. Whatever panoptic residues remain here – and Andrejevic does see such targets as being encouraged to self-discipline to become consistently conspicuous consumers – are to efficiently provide this elite with goods and services.

That said, the point of Gandy's (and Andrejevic's for that matter) work is to indicate that this is merely the mirror image of the negatively discriminatory activity implied by the 'panoptic sort'. Indeed Gandy's ongoing work pays less attention to the panoptic per se and focuses more on the statistical and software processes dedicated to 'rational discrimination'.[49] He notes that Geoff Bowker and Susan Leigh Star's work on *Sorting Things Out*[50] persuasively argues that organizational classification of users, clients, patients, consumers and so on is an increasingly significant part of modern life but fails to show how such classification not only describes but *also defines the possibilities for action* of affected groups. He goes on to insist that the 'rational discrimination' in economies of information is frequently based on racial profiling and eventuates in cumulative disadvantage to those thus negatively marked.

That is one example of ongoing theoretical panopticism. On the other hand, I refer you to work you have discussed in more than one place, on the 'synopticon', Thomas Mathiesen's neat neologism that contrasts the panopticon's 'few watching the many' with today's mass media, where as he puts it, 'the many watch the few'.[51] This hints at how the panoptic may actually find an ally in the mass media today. Mathiesen's key point, perhaps, is that whatever panoptic effects may still be present in today's societies, they cannot be understood in isolation from the synoptic, not least because they help to shape the effects of the latter. (This was seen vividly after 9/11, I think, when the constant TV replay of the blazing Twin Towers helped convey a sense of an ongoing imminent threat which, the authorities informed us *ad nauseam*, could be allayed by new security and surveillance measures.)[52]

Now, you use Mathiesen to support your case for the liquid modernity thesis and I agree; understanding the role of mass media is vital to our grasp of current cultural conditions. But surely Mathiesen tried to tell us that the panoptic works *with* the synoptic, not that the latter supersedes the former? So once again, I'd like you to respond to this – has the panoptic really shuffled off its mortal coil or is it still alive and well, albeit, perhaps, in its dotage? And there's a footnote to this as well. Aaron Doyle has pointed out recently (and rightly) that the model of 'media' used by Mathiesen is somewhat instrumental and top-down, and says little or nothing about resistance or about the ways that audiences decode media messages.[53] Also (though Mathiesen cannot fully be blamed for this, writing as he was before 'social media'), the synopticon seems unaware of the fragmentation of mass (TV) audiences or of the extensive influence of digital media today. Surely the media, including 'new media', may also be sites for questioning or for criticizing surveillance?

ZB Mathiesen's 'synopticon', in my reading, is a sort of 'DIY panopticon' which I already briefly discussed before – a panopticon significantly modified: surveillance without surveillors. As I see it, that neologism was coined by Mathiesen with an intention to grasp the impact exerted on surveillance by the much more general transformation taking place in managerial philosophy (myself, I dubbed that transformation, in my recent book on the collateral damage of inequality, 'the managerial revolution mark two'). What was previously viewed as the duty of the managers, to be attained at their expense and through their effort, has been ceded to the *objects* of management (or has been 'subsidiarized' to them, in the insinuation of another neologism, now commonly used to disguise or camouflage the zeal of managers to dump the control tasks they find cumbersome, inconvenient, unwieldy and vexingly constraining onto the shoulders of the controlled – and so to represent the burden-shifting as an endowment, an act of granting rights of autonomy and self-assertion, or even as the 'enablement' or 'resubjectivization' of formerly passive objects of managerial action). Allow me to restate here, in broad outlines, what in my view 'the managerial revolution mark two' is about.[54]

In its original sense bequeathed by the times when the ideal of the industrial process was conceived on the pattern of a homeostatic machine going through pre-designed and strictly repetitive motions and kept on a steady, immutable course, managing people was indeed a chore. It required meticulous regimentation and close and continuous panopticon-style surveillance. It needed the imposition of a monotonous routine, bound to stultify the creative impulses of *both* the managed and their managers. It generated boredom and a constantly seething resentment threatening to self-combust into an open conflict. It was also a costly way of 'getting things done': instead of enlisting the non-regimented potentials of hired labour in the service of the job, it used precious resources to stifle them, excise them and keep them out of mischief. All in all, day-to-day management was not the kind of task that resourceful people, people in power, were likely to relish and cherish: they were not going to perform it a moment longer than they had to, and given the power resources at their disposal they could not be expected to put off that moment for long. And they did not.

The current 'great transformation mark two' (to borrow Karl Polanyi's memorable phrase), the emergence of the widely lauded and welcome 'experience economy' drawing on the totality of personality resources, warts and all, signals that this moment of 'emancipation of the managers from the burden of managing' has arrived. Using James Burnham's terms, one could describe it as the 'managerial revolution mark two'; though, as revolutions go, there was little or no change in the incumbents of power and office. What has happened – what is happening – is more a coup d'état than a revolution: a proclamation from the top that the old game has been abandoned and that new rules of the game are in force. The people who initiated and saw through the revolution remained at the helm – and, if anything, settled into their offices even more securely than before. This revolution was started and conducted in the name of adding to their power, further strengthening their grip, and immunizing their domination against the resentment and rebellion that the form of their domination, before the revolution, used to generate. Since the second managerial revolution, the power of the managers has been reinforced and made well-nigh invulnerable by cutting off most of the restraining and otherwise inconvenient strings previously attached to it. During that second revolution, the managers

banished the pursuit of routine and invited the forces
of spontaneity to occupy the now vacant supervisors'
rooms. They refused to manage; instead, they demanded
self-management from the residents, on the threat of
eviction. The right to extend the residential lease was
subjected to recurrent competition: after each round,
the most playful and the best performing win the next
term's lease, though without a guarantee, or even an
increased likelihood, of emerging unscathed from the
next test. On the walls of the banqueting suite of the
'experience economy' the reminder that 'you are as
good as your *last* success' (but not as your last but one)
has replaced the inscription of 'mene, tekel, upharsin'
('counted, weighed, allocated'). Favouring subjectivity,
playfulness and performativity, the organizations of the
era of the 'experience economy' have to, want to and do
prohibit long-term planning and the accumulation of
merits. This indeed will keep the residents constantly on
the move and busy – in the feverish search for ever new
evidence that they are still welcome . . .

'Synopticon' serves that new demand very well, thank
you. With the synopticon replacing the panopticon,
there is no need to build heavy walls and erect watchtowers to keep the inmates inside, while hiring countless
throngs of supervisors to make sure they stick to the
prescribed routine (at an additional cost of placating
the simmering wrath and unwillingness to cooperate
that monotonous routine usually breeds, as well as the
cost of having to make a continuous effort to nip in the
bud the menace of a rebellion against the indignity of
servitude). It is the objects of the managerial discipli-
nary concerns who are now expected to self-discipline
and bear the material and psychical costs of discipline

production. They are expected to erect the walls themselves and stay in them of their own volition. With the
carrot (or its promise) replacing the stick, temptation
and seduction taking over the functions once performed
by normative regulation, and the grooming and honing
of desires substituting for costly and dissent-generating
policing, the watchtowers (like the rest of the strategy
aimed at eliciting desirable and eliminating undesirable
conduct) have been privatized, while the procedure of
issuing permissions for wall-building has been deregulated. Instead of necessity chasing its victims, it is now
the task of the volunteers to chase the opportunities of
servitude (the concept of 'voluntary servitude' coined by
Étienne de la Boétie had to wait four centuries before it
turned into the objective of common managerial practice). Have you noticed, by the way, that in every round
of corporate 'expenditure cutting', it is 'middle management' (that is, the former supervisors of the rank and
file) who are first for the chop?

The gear for the assembly of DIY, mobile and
portable, single-person mini-panopticons is of course
commercially supplied. It is the would-be inmates who
bear responsibility for choosing and purchasing the gear,
assembling it and putting it into operation. Though the
monitoring, collating and processing of the volatile distribution of individual synoptical initiatives once again
requires professionals; but it is the 'users' of the services
of Google or Facebook who produce the 'database' – the
raw material which professionals remould into Gandy's
'targeted categories' of prospective buyers – through
their scattered, apparently autonomous yet synoptically
pre-coordinated actions. To avoid confusion, therefore,
I would rather abstain from using the term 'panopticon'

in this context. The professionals in question are anything but the old-fashioned surveillors watching over the monotony of the binding routine; they are rather trackers or stalkers of the exquisitely changeable patterns of desires and of the conduct inspired by those volatile desires. They are, so to speak, the 'finishing branch' of the synopticon already in operation and not of their design and build. Or perhaps those engineers employed in 'database processing' are located somewhere between synopticon and ban-opticon, in as far as the products of their labour form a necessary condition of the profitable deployment of ban-optical techniques in marketing. It is so and it must be so, considering that any effective marketing requires knowledge of constituencies unfit for targeting as much as it needs reconnaissance of the most promising 'targets' of commercial efforts. Effective marketing needs *both* synopticon *and* ban-opticon. The 'data processing engineers' provide the communication channel linking the two.

A good, indeed an archetypal example of the interface between those two types of institutionalized surveilling techniques is the software developed for the use of corporations needing to process incoming calls. That software allows callers to be sorted out and set apart for differentiated treatment – according to the promise they show (or for that matter don't show) for enhancing the company's profits. The promising ones are not kept on hold but immediately connected to senior operators entitled to take decisions on the spot. The hopeless ones are, on the other hand, kept waiting endlessly, fed with boringly repetitive messages interspersed with tunes replayed *ad nauseam* as well as recorded promises to be connected to the first available operator. If the intruder survives the treatment and the derision it implies, and refuses to hang up, she or he is connected in the end to a lower rank operator not empowered to settle the problem (normally a grievance) that was the reason for the call.

3

Remoteness, distancing and automation

David Lyon One of the most striking things made possible by the twentieth century's astonishing technological development is the vastly increased capacity to act at a distance. Even this conversation we're having is electronically enabled. We don't have to wait for the opportunity for an intercontinental trip, or even for the ten days it would take for a letter to travel each way across the Atlantic, to discuss in this way. We simply write our messages and flick them effortlessly over massive spaces, wait a few hours or a few days, and the response pops up in the inbox. Of course, because I know you, I can hear your voice in my head as I read the next segment, and because I know the room where you're writing and I'm aware of what other responsibilities you have on your plate right now, I can imagine you at work as you re-enter the space of our dialogue. But what does this doing-things-at-a-distance mean in the context of liquid surveillance?

Earlier, we spoke of drones, those mechanical dragonflies that peer and pry where other eyes can't see (not forgetting their deadlier big cousins whose task is rather to kill, cleanly, in places where armed forces cannot, or better, prefer not to go). You spoke of the 'comfortable invisibility' of these eyes in the skies and the exempting from responsibility of their masters, who program them to fly their own itineraries and time their own image-capture. And you reminded us of the indirect effect that those countries or states using such at-a-distance technologies thereby also distance themselves from the conflicts, crimes or crises they are supposed to detect or deter.

In the years when you were settling in Leeds, I was a graduate student grappling with the grim questions raised by my undergraduate immersion in the worlds of modern European history, ideas and literature. My deepest perplexity, I think, concerned the Holocaust, and we even visited a number of sites – Dachau, Ravensbruck, Mauthausen, Auschwitz – to see those fateful railway tracks and orderly buildings whose calculated purpose was exacting forced labour, or human experimentation and extermination. Although I was a keen reader of your work from the late 1970s on, I must say that, when it appeared in 1989, I found *Modernity and the Holocaust* peculiarly profound and moving. It was a watershed.

I started to suspect that its haunting themes spoke not only to modern bureaucracy but also to *la technique* in Jacques Ellul's sense and to various specific technologies and technological systems that were challenging aspects of the then novel 'information revolution'. I could discern from what you were saying some extensions in new and technologically enhanced organizational practices and, eventually, to more ubiquitous surveillance. The meticulous organization, the careful separation of the official from the 'victim', and the mechanical efficiency of the operation – noted in the Preface – are indeed now devoted, not to physical violence, but to the sorting of populations into categories for differential treatment. The pattern is parallel, even if the effects – being selected for certain death or for social disadvantage – are far from comparable. But in an adiaphorized context, the pattern or process, prized for its efficiency, may have effects ranging from economic relegation to the periphery to extraordinary rendition to a rogue power.

So may I begin this part of our conversation with a more general question about the elaboration and enhancement of the kinds of bureaucratic rationalities visible in those 1930s death factories and labour camps in current organizational patterns and, of course, surveillance practices? This is not for a moment meant in macabre, alarmist or anachronistic ways. And as always, detailed accounts, not just abstract assertions, are vital for full analysis. I want us to get at the underlying motifs, the abiding configurations of imagination and accomplishment, seen especially in the concepts – or rather practices – of distancing, remoteness, automation. How far are such connections constructive and illuminating, in your view?

Zygmunt Bauman   I assume, though I can't prove (as, I believe, no one can), that over the millennia following Eve managing to tempt Adam into tasting a fruit of the Tree of Knowledge of Good and Evil, human capacities and propensities to do good and human inclinations and abilities to do evil have stayed roughly unchanged; it was just that the opportunities and/or the pressures to do good or evil varied – in parallel with the settings of human togetherness and prevailing patterns of human interaction. What look like and tend to be described as cases of unloading and letting loose the evil instincts of humans, or on the contrary suppressing them or smothering and choking them down, are better understood as the products of a social (and, as a rule, power-assisted) 'manipulation of probabilities' (increasing the probability of certain types of conduct, while decreasing the likelihood of some others). The manipulation (rearrangement, redistribution) of probabilities is the ultimate meaning of all 'order building', and more generally of all 'structuring' of an amorphous field of random ('chaotic') occurrences; and the prevailing models of 'order', as well as the most sought-after patterns of 'structure', change in history – though, contrary to what the common view of 'progress' implies, in a pendulum-like fashion, and in anything but a uniform and coordinated way.

The demons haunting and harrowing the twentieth century were gestated in the course of the resolute efforts to complete the task aimed at by the modern era from its very beginning (indeed, the task whose assumption defined that beginning, having triggered the mode of life called 'modern', which means in a nutshell a state of compulsive, obsessive and addictive 'modernization'). The task set for each successive area or round of modernization, yet hardly ever seen through to the end (if reaching such an end was ever feasible), was to impose a transparent and manageable design over unruly and uncontrollable chaos: to bring the world of humans, hitherto vexingly opaque, bafflingly unpredictable and infuriatingly disobedient and oblivious to human wishes and objectives, into order: a *complete, incontestable* and *unchallenged* order. Order under the indomitable rule of Reason.

That Reason, which had its cradle in Francis Bacon's 'Solomon's House' in his *New Atlantis*, spent its apprenticeship years in Jeremy Bentham's panopticon, and just at the threshold of our lifetime settled in the innumerable factory buildings haunted by the ghosts of Frederick Winslow Taylor's 'time and motion measurements', by the spectre of Henry Ford's 'conveyor belt', and by the phantom of le Corbusier's idea of home as a 'machine for living'. That Reason assumed the variety and divergence of human intentions and preferences to be but temporary irritants, bound to be pushed out of the way of the order-building enterprise through skilful manipulation of behavioural probabilities via a proper arrangement of external settings and through rendering impotent and irrelevant any features resisting such manipulation. Jeremy Bentham's late eighteenth-century vision of universal surveillance was eventually elevated by Michel Foucault and his countless disciples and followers to the rank of the universal pattern of power and domination, and ultimately of all social order.

Order of that sort meant, ultimately, the absence of anything 'redundant' – useless or undesirable, in other words – of anything that caused unhappiness or was confusing and/or discomforting, because it stood in the way of full and undisturbed control over the human condition. It meant, in short, rendering the permissible obligatory – and eliminating all the rest. The conviction that such a feat is plausible, feasible, in sight and within human reach, as well as the irresistible urge to act on that conviction, was and remains the defining attribute of modernity; it reached its peak with the dawn of the twentieth century. The 'classic modern era', brutally challenged and stripped of self-confidence by the outbreak of the Great War and ushered by it into a half-century of agony, was a journey towards *perfection* – to reach a state in which the strains of making things better would grind to a halt, as any further interference with the shape of the human world could only make it worse. For the same reasons, the modern era was also an era of *destruction*. Striving towards perfection called for eradicating, wiping out and getting rid of innumerable beings unlikely to be accommodated in a perfect scheme of things. *Destruction was the very substance of creation*: the destruction of imperfections was the condition – a sufficient as much as a necessary condition – of the way being paved to perfection. The story of modernity, and particularly of its twentieth-century denouement, was the chronicle of creative destruction. The atrocities marking the course of that 'short century' (as Eric Hobsbawm dubbed it, fixing its genuine starting point at 1914 and true ending at 1989) were born of the dream of the neatness, purity, clarity and transparency of ultimate perfection.

Attempts to make that dream come true were too numerous to be listed here. Two among them stand out from the rest, however, due to their unprecedented scale of ambition and uncanny resoluteness. Both deserve to be counted among the fullest and most dazzling renditions of the dream of 'ultimate order': a kind of order that has no need of and does not allow further reorderings. It was against the standards they set that all other attempts, genuine or putative, undertaken, intended or suspected, came to be measured – and it is their bland and uncompromising thoroughness that still lurks in our collective memory as the prototype of all subsequent instances of following suit – however blunt or disguised, however determined or half-hearted. The two attempts in question are, of course, the Nazi and the Communist undertakings to eradicate once and for all, wholesale and in one fell swoop, every disorderly, opaque, random, control-resisting element or aspect of the human condition.

Nazi-inspired exercises were conducted in the very heart of European civilization, science and art – in lands priding themselves on having come closest to fulfilling Francis Bacon's dream of 'Solomon's House': a world under the undivided and unchallenged rule of reason, itself the most loyal servant of human beings' best interests, comfort and happiness. The idea of tidying up the world through excising and burning out its impurities, as well as the conviction that it was feasible (provided power and will were mustered adequate to the task), was hatched in Hitler's mind while he was strolling along the streets of Vienna, at that time the veritable capital of European science and arts.

At approximately the same time, at the 'limen' of European modernity, a kindred idea was gestated in the minds of people gazing piously, with a mixture of respect and jealousy, at the other side of the porous border, awestruck by what they saw: the Communist idea of chasing, catching up with and overtaking modern civilization along the racetrack leading towards perfection. The humiliating awareness of having been left behind in that chase encouraged urgency, prompted haste and suggested a short-cut strategy; it implied the need to condense into the lifespan of a single generation what on the other side of the liminal threshold would have taken a long string of generations to accomplish. And there was of course a huge price to be paid in the pains of the generation chosen to usher in the pain-free world. No sacrifice was deemed excessive when it was viewed against the charms and nobility of the destination. And no part of extant reality could claim immunity or safe passage on grounds of its past merits, let alone its mere presence in the world. The entry ticket to the world of perfection had to be earned anew. And, of course, not everybody had the right to line up for tickets: just as with any other model of a brave new world, the Communist model would not be completed without an inventory of those disqualified and refused entry.

Having thoroughly scrutinized the archives of the research units and administrative offices of the Nazi establishment, Götz Aly and Susanne Heim insist that the 'policy of modernization' and the 'policy of destruction' were intimately connected in the Nazi policies aimed at redrawing the political, ethnic and social map of Europe. The Nazi rulers were determined to enforce in Europe, after its military conquest, 'new political, economic and social structures, as speedily as possible'.[55] This intention meant, of course, that reckoning with such historical accidents as the geographic location of ethnic settlements and the resulting distribution of natural resources and labour forces was not on; the essence of power is, after all, the capacity to ignore such whims of fortune. In a world constructed to order, in a pre-planned and pre-designed, rational fashion, there will be no room for many of the leftovers of a haphazard past which might be unfit or downright damaging for the newly installed order of things. Some populations might need to be deported to other locations, where their capacities could be put to better use and harnessed to other undertakings.

It was because of their extreme nature, their uninhibited and untamed radicalism, their resolution to pull out all the stops that the concentration camps and the Gulag, Auschwitz and Kolyma, and, taken as a whole, the Nazi and Communist episodes of modern history with which they are associated, have been widely though wrongly viewed as rebellions against, rather than loyal to, the essential precepts of 'modern civilization'. Instead, they brought to its ultimate consequences the logic of the modern passion for order-building – which otherwise stopped short of reaching its full potential and acquiring a volume of might and a degree of mastery over nature and history to match the dreams and ambitions of the modern spirit. But they only did what others were also willing, yet too shy (or too wan, or not resolute enough) to do . . .

And what we go on doing, even though in a less spectacular and therefore less repellent, more diluted and attenuated rendition – we do, as you've so rightly pinpointed, through faithfully following the precept of 'distancing, remoteness, automation'. We do it now, in other words, in a high-tech fashion, having transcended, rejected and by and large left behind the primitive, cottage-industry methods that used moral preaching to get people to do things they would rather not be doing, used weak and unreliable human eyes for surveillance, brainwashing to gain discipline and police to ensure it lasted. Plus the elimination of defective (*unwerte*) individuals and categories, as economists, agronomists and planners of public spaces felt themselves obliged to 'sanitize the social structure' of the conquered lands. The racial quality of humans, according to the Nazi social engineers, could only be improved by the annihilation or at least castration of *unwertes Leben*.[56]

DL Yes, modernity, it seems, has much to answer for. Or should we rather say that modernity reveals some of its profoundly unattractive faces in your account of how technical ambitions can silence the voice of conscience and compassion? Perhaps even more fearful, though, is that despite the postwar hand-wringing over the Holocaust, so little seems to have been learned. Rightful regret and condemnation of specific regimes seems almost superficial beside the ongoing drive to decouple technique from its proper bounds. The idolatry that binds us to its logic and blinds us to its limits makes those distancing effects even more pervasive and pernicious in the 'age of information'.

ZB Hans Jonas, one of the greatest twentieth-century ethical philosophers, was arguably the first to bring to our attention, and with a bluntness that left nothing to the imagination, the gruesome consequence of the modern victory of technology over ethics. We now possess technology, he said (note, he said that well before the ideas, let alone the technologies, of smart missiles or drones were born), with which we can act at distances so enormous (both in space and time) that they cannot be embraced by our ethical imagination, still confined as it had been for centuries to those narrow spaces 'within sight' and 'within reach'. And Ellul, whom you aptly recall, threw a shadow over the prospect of ever bridging the widening technology–ethics gap by observing that the 'instrumentality' of our rationality has been reversed since Max Weber's time: it no longer guides us to adjust means to ends, but allows our ends to be determined by the available means.

We no longer develop techniques 'in order to' do what we want to be done, but we select things for doing just because the technology for doing them has been developed (or, rather, has been come across; accidentally – 'serendipitously' – found). And the greater the distance at which technology allows us to cause things to appear or disappear, the lower the chance that the new opportunities enabled by technology will be left lying fallow, not to mention be barred from deployment just because their potential outcomes or collateral effects might clash with some other (including moral) considerations irrelevant to the task at hand. In other words, the most seminal effect of progress in the technology of 'distancing, remoteness, automation' is the *progressive and perhaps unstoppable liberation of our actions from moral constraints.* When the principle of 'we can do it, so we will do it' rules our choices, we reach a point at which moral responsibility for human deeds and their inhuman effects can neither be authoritatively posited nor effectively executed.

During the last world war, George Orwell mused: 'As I write, highly civilized human beings are flying overhead, trying to kill me. They do not feel any enmity against me as an individual, nor I against them. They are "only doing their duty", as the saying goes.' A few years later, scanning the vast multitiered graveyard called Europe in search of the kind of humans who managed to do that to other humans, Hannah Arendt laid bare the 'floating' habit of responsibility inside the bureaucratic body; she named the consequences of this floating the 'responsibility of nobody'. More than half a century later, we could say much the same of the current state of the killing arts.

Continuity, then? Oh yes, there is continuity, though true to continuity's habits, in company with a few discontinuities . . . The major novelty is the effacing of differences of status between means and ends. Or, rather, a war of independence ending in the victory of the axes over the axemen. It is now the axes who select the ends: the heads to be axed. The axemen can do little more to stop them (that is, to change the minds which they do not have or appeal to the feelings which they do not possess) than could the legendary sorcerer's apprentice (this allegory is by no means fanciful: as the military experts Thom Shanker and Matt Richtel put it in the *New York Times*, 'just as the military has long pushed technology forward, it is now at the forefront in figuring out how humans can cope with technology without being overwhelmed by it'. And as the neuroscientist Art Kramer sees the situation in the same article, 'there is information overload at every level of the military – from the general to the soldier on the ground.'[57] Everybody in the army, 'from the general to the soldier on the ground', has been demoted from the sorcerer's office to the lowly rank of his apprentice.

Since 11 September 2001, the amount of 'intelligence' gathered by the cutting-edge technology at the US Army's disposal has risen 1,600 per cent. It is not that the axemen have lost their conscience or have been immunized against moral scruples; they simply can't cope with the volumes of information amassed by the gadgets they operate. The gadgets, as a matter of fact, can now do as well (or as badly . . .) *with* or *without* their help, thank you. Kick the axemen away from their screens, and you'd hardly notice their absence when you look at the distribution of results.

By the start of the twenty-first century, military technology had managed to float and so 'depersonalize' responsibility to an extent unimaginable in Orwell's or Arendt's time. 'Smart', 'intelligent' missiles and 'drones' have taken over decision-making and the selection of targets from both the rank-and-file and the highest placed ranks in the military machine. I would suggest that the most seminal technological developments in recent years have not been sought and accomplished in relation to the murderous powers of weapons, but in the area of the 'adiaphorization' of military killing (that is, removal from the category of acts subject to moral evaluation). As Günther Anders warned after Nagasaki but still well before Vietnam, Afghanistan or Iraq, 'you don't gnash your teeth when you press a button . . . A key is a key.' Whether pressing a key starts a contraption to make ice-cream, feeds current into an electricity network, or lets loose the Horsemen of the Apocalypse makes no difference. 'The gesture that will initiate the Apocalypse will not differ from any of the other gestures – and it will be performed, like all other identical gestures, by a similarly routine-guided and routine-bored operator'.[58] 'If something symbolizes the satanic nature of our situation, it is precisely that innocence of the gesture,' Anders concludes: the negligibility of the effort and thought needed to set off a cataclysm – *any* cataclysm, including 'globocide' . . .

What is new is the 'drone', aptly called 'predator', which has taken over the task of gathering and processing information. The electronic equipment of the drone excels in performing its task. But what task? Just as the manifest function of an axe is to enable an axeman to execute a convict, the manifest function of a drone is to enable its operator to locate the object of an execution. But the drone that excels in that function and keeps flooding the operator with tides of information he is unable to digest, let alone process promptly and swiftly, 'in real time', may be performing another, latent and unspoken function: to exonerate the operator of the moral guilt that would haunt him were he fully and truly in charge of selecting the convicts for execution; and, more importantly still, to reassure the operator in advance that if a mistake happens, it won't be blamed on his immorality. If 'innocent people' are killed, it is a technical fault, not a moral failure or sin – and, judging from the statute books, most certainly not a crime. As Shanker and Richtel put it, 'drone-based sensors have given rise to a new class of wired warriors who must filter the information sea. But sometimes they are drowning.' But is not the capacity to drown the operator's mental (and so, obliquely but inevitably, moral) faculties included in the drone's design? Is not drowning the operator the drone's paramount function? When in February 2011, twenty-three Afghan wedding guests were killed, the button-pushing operators could blame it on the screens that had turned into 'drool buckets': they got lost just by staring into them. There were children among the bomb victims, but the operators 'did not adequately focus on them amid the swirl of data' – 'much like a cubicle worker who loses track of an important e-mail under the mounting pile'. Well, no one would accuse such a cubicle worker of a moral failure . . .

Starting off a cataclysm – including, as Anders insists, 'globocide' – has now become even easier and more plausible than it used to be when Anders wrote down his warnings. The 'routine-bored operator' has been joined by his colleague and his probable replacement and successor – the chap with his eyes fixed on a 'drool bucket', his mind drowning in a 'swirl of data' . . .

DL I agree with you substantially, Zygmunt. There are important continuities to be borne in mind (along with some discontinuities, amplifications and diminutions) in the world of what might be called action-in-absentia. However, while your examples are chilling, I'd like us to reflect a little more on the non-military continuities, the ones that don't directly involve killing. Some surveillance contexts do produce death as expected or risked outcomes, but the vast majority do not. However, the adiaphorization to which you refer may very well be evident even though the character of the missing moral responsibility may differ.

Let me connect again with some of your own comments on surveillance, this time in the context of globalization. Some may wish to quibble or carp about your 'globals and locals' or 'tourists and vagabonds' distinctions but the point you made in your 1998 title *Globalization* still holds – that the database is a major means of sieving or filtering out the unwanted from the wanted, the desirable migrants from the undesirable. Those databases enable 'doing things at a distance' (or action-in-absentia) no less than in the cases that you've just been commenting on so poignantly. Relatedly, in my own work I've drawn attention to the fact that if we're thinking of migrant populations, the borders are everywhere.[59]

I mean by this several things, but two stand out. On

the one hand, the border as a geographical line makes even less sense than it did when it was conceived as a sort of physical expression of a mapping practice. Although the paraphernalia of checkpoints or Customs and Immigration offices may be at border crossings, the use of remote databases and telecommunications networks means that the crucial – and consequential – checking happens extraterritorially or at least in multiple locations whose actual whereabouts is immaterial (almost in both senses!). But another meaning of the border being everywhere is that it doesn't matter either where the 'undesirable' migrant is. You can be apprehended anywhere (indeed I noticed a case in the UK this week where immigration officers were checking people on public transport networks, in bus stations in fact, in a somewhat elastic interpretation of the rules that supposedly govern them).[60]

What I'm driving at is that the business of doing things at a distance that Jonas, Levinas and others wrote about has now been massively expanded. This capacity for remote action enabled by information infrastructures and sorting software is indeed implicated in military decision-making but it's also a feature of all manner of decision-making that is highly consequential for the life chances and opportunities of many populations. Can we introduce the critique of adiaphorization in these contexts as well? Does pursuing these questions seem to you to be a worthwhile strategy?

ZB Every and any kind and instance of surveillance serves the same purpose: spotting the targets, location of targets and/or focusing on targets – all functional differentiation starts from that common ground.

You are of course right when you observe that focusing on the 'order to kill' narrows our topic; though I suppose and suspect that R&D related to and financed by the military with 'distant execution' in mind is the 'advance unit' of the surveillance army, supplying most of the technological innovations later adapted to the needs of other, paramilitary 'securitarian' varieties of surveillance – and also for downright commercial, marketing uses. I would suggest as well that the pioneering military applications set the technical standards for the contents of the surveillance toolbox, as well as the cognitive and pragmatic frame for their deployment; I also guess that this is more true in the era of the ban-opticon than at any other time.

Yes, you are right again – instruments of surveillance installed at the entrances of shops or gated communities are not equipped with an 'executive arm' designed to annihilate the spotted and pinpointed targets – but their purpose, all the same, is the targets' incapacitation and removal 'beyond bounds'. The same might be said of the surveillance used to pick out the credit-unworthy from among aspiring clients, or of the surveillance tools used to set apart the penniless loiterers from the promising clients among the crowds flooding the shopping malls. Neither of those two varieties of contemporary surveillance has the purpose of causing physical death; and yet what they are after is a sort of death (the death of everything that matters). It is not a corporeal demise, and moreover not finite but (in principle) revocable: it is a *social* death, leaving open, so to speak, the chance of a *social* resurrection (rehabilitation, a restoration to rights). Social exclusion, the raison d'être of the ban-opticon, is in its essence analogous to a verdict of social *death*, even if in the great majority of cases the sentence entails a stay of execution.

And you are also absolutely on target when you note that the capacity offered by technology of surveillance at a distance (in other words, rendering the span of surveillance fully and truly extraterritorial, free from the limits and constraints imposed by geographic distance) is deployed with exceptional zeal in controlling migration, an eminently *global* process. I agree with every word of your analysis. The United States moved its immigration officers from the landing points of incoming flights to the boarding points; however, this looks like a primitive, cottage-industry solution compared with the fast-spreading methods of governments of affluent countries, the potential destinations of migrants, to 'nip the menace in the bud' – retargeting surveilling gear on the *starting* points of migration instead of its presumed and feared *destinations*; spotting, arresting and immobilizing suspects well away from their own borders, and blackmailing or bribing labour-exporting countries into accepting the role of police precincts engaged in (read, responsible for) the jobs of 'crime prevention' or the 'incarceration and disabling of suspects'.

We can say that what is involved here is not so much stripping physical distance of its importance and overcoming its potential to resist and obstruct, as the manipulation of distances. The distance between migrants' point of departure and the point of their arrival is extended beyond its 'specific span' (migrants are put in the category of 'crime suspects' far away from the place where an actual breach of the law might occur and recast them as law-breakers), whereas the physical distance separating the watchtowers from their objects of surveillance is drastically reduced to nil through the electronic tools of 'real-time communication'.

A collateral gain of the surveillors – a bonus whose attraction is not to be underestimated, a temptation hardly to be resisted – is the chance to 'cover up' or 'clean up' the odious and condemnable effects of such manipulation, with its potential to backfire: the counterfactual, geographical and legal distancing of the sites where the inevitably unwholesome 'dirty job' of execution is performed from the offices gathering the intelligence and giving the command. In other words, to invoke Hannah Arendt, the 'floating' of responsibility. It is an expedient practised by the perpetrators of the Holocaust to awesome effect long before the arrival of today's sophisticated technology of surveillance, but one which that arrival has rendered so much neater, smoother, more trouble-free (for the givers of orders) and more proficient. And as we already know, setting responsibility afloat is one of the widespread and effective stratagems of *adiaphorization* – of disabling moral resistance against the committing of immoral deeds and the sole use of criteria of instrumental efficiency in the choice of ways to proceed.

DL Can we just clarify one thing, please, Zygmunt? When you speak of technology's 'effects' it sometimes sounds as if they are always and everywhere negative. New technologies drive a wedge between human beings and their moral responsibilities to each other just as, perhaps, bureaucracy did before them. So drones assist in killing at a distance, as other electronic machines in general enable action-in-absentia. And it does seem, according to the reported studies, that only a minority of drone operators (for example) suffer from post-traumatic stress disorder, even though the video feed they must watch is often horrendously detailed.[61]

My question is, does it have to be this way? Is there something ineluctable about the baleful effects of electronic mediation or can the same technologies also facilitate humane and hopeful social relationships? The question was already implicitly present in the way I initiated this conversation, observing that to engage in an intercontinental dialogue like this is only possible because of information and communication technologies, or what we now tend to call new media.

I am not, of course, proposing technologies as some sort of 'neutral' tools whose moral direction is revealed only in what they are 'used for'. All technological development is surely the product of cultural, social and political relationships. All that we dub 'technology' is more properly a feature of 'techno-social' or 'socio-technical' relations. In this sense, all technological gadgets and systems exhibit moral tendencies; not moral behaviour as such (in my view) but moral direction. If this is correct, then engaged in one way, technologies may contribute to negative distancing effects, but in another to at least a partial overcoming of geographical distance. My enjoyment of Skyping with distant children or grandchildren is a case in point.

Media theorist Roger Silverstone used to lament the fact that two understandings of distance tend to be conflated in our references to technologies, moral and geographical. He speaks of 'proper distance', by which he means 'distinctive, correct and morally or socially appropriate' distance and he proposes that this term be applied critically.[62] What is the proper distance for internet or for surveillance relationships? To provide the means of communicating over distance is to promote connection, perhaps even communication, but the spatial and the social should not be elided. Distance is also a moral category and to overcome it one needs proximity, not technology. This is of course close to what you've said elsewhere, for instance in *Postmodern Ethics* (1993), that proximity is the realm of intimacy and morality; distance that of estrangement and law.

For you, I think, modernity refuses the intimate and the moral and this refusal is all too often imposed on us through law and state activities, and, I would add, including surveillance especially. Proximity and proper distance require responsibility, which is so often denied by modernity and technology. But Silverstone's proper distance is nuanced. Technology does not determine things in his view; it constrains but may also enable. In the flux and fluidity of relationships, a range of technological and discursive mediations destabilize the proper distance needed to act ethically. Proper distance has to be produced. I have argued for a long time that while much surveillance is bound up with motifs of control – power is always implicated – this does not exclude the possibility that there are ways in which surveillance may be in the service of care for the Other. The key question here is how we can behave responsibly towards mediated others.

So, back to my question, can surveillance technologies be tuned to the key of care or are they hopelessly compromised with the disabling of morality and adiaphorization?

ZB We can think of modernity (which, in the last account, is a state of compulsive, obsessive and addictive 'modernization', a code word for making things better than they are) as a sword with its sharp edge constantly pressed against extant realities. We can think in the same way about technology – as the invention, development and deployment of techniques appropriate for that task is a major, arguably the paramount tool of modern purposeful activity, it can be seen as modernity's defining attribute. But swords are usually double-edged; they are usefully applied to deal with the task at hand, but they can cut both ways, and swinging swords are by their nature dangerous tools to use. Apart from their intended goals, chosen for their assumed propriety and goodness, they are known to hurt and damage unintended targets. Purposeful action needs to be focused on the issue at hand in order to be effective; but the objects of action are as a rule locked into loops of interdependence with numerous other objects that are left out of focus on that occasion.

So alongside the appointed objectives, actions inevitably have 'unanticipated consequences'; harmful side-effects no one desired, and most certainly no one planned. Ulrich Beck famously suggested that every and any action involves 'risks', and that the 'positive' effect of action and its 'negative' side-effect stem from the same causes and so one can't be had without the other. Accepting an action, we are bound by the same token to accept the risks with which it is inseparably associated. Recently, the discourse of 'risks' has tended to be displaced and replaced by the discourse of 'collateral damage' or 'collateral casualties' – the idea of 'collaterality' suggesting that the assumed positive effects and admittedly negative ones run in parallel, and for that reason each conscious, outspoken application of any novel technique opens (in principle at least) a new area of previously unexperienced fatalities. Having invented and built the railway network, our ancestors invented railway catastrophes. The introduction of air travel opened a vast field of previously unheard-of air disasters. The technology of atomic/nuclear energy brought us Chernobyl and Fukushima, the never exorcised spectre of a nuclear war. Genetic engineering has already radically increased the quantities of food available, while never ceasing to be a global catastrophe waiting to happen in the event some designer species set up unplanned interactions and trigger unintended processes which run out of control . . .

Silverstone, I gather, speaks of the same inseparable attribute of 'technological progress', only in his case it is presented in 'a reverse order', so to speak. He would, I guess, wholeheartedly agree with the critique of the intended applications of surveillance, and view iniquitous objectives as a major reason and engine behind the spectacular progress in surveilling technology; his 'discovery' is that a technology aimed at disablement may have some uses for the seekers of enablement as well (as walls are used to build ghettoes and prisons as well as to serve seekers of niches of solidarity and community feelings). That technology is a double-edged sword, and that it may find unprognosticated applications and serve unplanned interests, is hardly a discovery, however. However numerous the instances of praiseworthy (yet surely unplanned) applications of surveillance techniques might be, the fact remains that it is not those meritorious and approvable uses that set the pattern and draw the 'road map' of surveillance technology development; neither do they decide the social and ethical value of that technology. Even if the favourable news multiplies, there is still – as Ulrich Beck keeps reminding us – the imperative of careful and conscientious 'risk calculation'. A calculation of gains and losses. What prevails on balance, taking all impacts into account – social gains or losses? The advancement of morality or moral devastation? The promotion of social division and separation, or the enhancement of human solidarity? No one denies that as the supplies of non-renewable sources of energy rapidly run out, atomic energy may offer a genuine solution to the impending energy crisis. And yet, after Fukushima, governments of the most powerful lands are seriously considering the possibility of a total ban on atomic energy plants . . .

4
In/security and surveillance

David Lyon Among the rationales for engaging in surveillance, a key motif today is procuring security. As with much surveillance, of course, this is nothing new. Think of biblical references to the importance of a 'watch' being kept over the city, or Francisco on guard at the entrance to Elsinore castle in the opening scene in Shakespeare's *Hamlet*. Maintaining security has always provided a rationale for keeping an alert watch, for identifying those who would pass as friend or foe. And as such it certainly appears to have a strong protective motif, watching-to-care-for.

In the twenty-first century, however, such innocence seems in short supply. Security – by which is often meant some ill-defined idea of 'national' security – is today a political priority in and across many countries, and of course it is a massive motivator in the world of surveillance. The prominent means of procuring security, it seems, are new surveillance techniques and technologies, which are supposed to guard us, not against distinct dangers, but against rather more shadowy and shapeless risks. Things have changed, for both watchers and the watched. If once you could sleep easy knowing that the night watch was at the city gate, the same cannot be said of today's 'security'. It seems that, ironically, today's security generates forms of *in*security as a by-product – or maybe in some cases as a deliberate policy? – an insecurity felt keenly by the very people that security measures are supposed to protect.

Now, you have commented that liquid modern society is a 'contraption attempting to make life with fear liveable'.[63] So far from modernity managing to conquer fears one by one, liquid modernity now discovers that struggling against fears is a lifelong task. And if we in the West weren't fully conscious of this before 9/11, what you call the 'terrors of the global' caught up with us then. After 9/11 the practices of risk management, already de rigueur for several decades, became well known, obvious. And again, you observed that with the surveillant focus on 'external, visible and recordable objects', new surveillance systems were also bound to be 'oblivious to the individual motives and choices behind the recorded images, and so must lead eventually to the substitution of the idea of "suspicious categories" in place of individual evildoers'.[64]

Little wonder, then, that *in*securities appear just as fast as each new full body scanner or biometric fingerprint machine is installed in the airport, or as upgraded passports with built-in radio frequency identification tags are required at border crossings. There's no knowing when the categories of risk may 'accidentally' include us or, more accurately, exclude us from participation, entry or entitlement. Or it may just be that what you rightly dub the 'security obsession' produces more mundane unease. Katja Franko Aas and others tell of the Norwegian airline carriers who wrote to airport authorities complaining of 'excessive security' that was damaging actual air security. Air crews felt harassed by being checked ten or twelve times a day. Pilots with hundreds of passengers in their care couldn't be trusted to take a lunch break without a security check. They said they 'felt like criminals'.[65]

But it would be misleading to imagine that the *in*securities associated with surveillance-in-the-service-of-security are limited to directly post-9/11 matters. For example, Torin Monahan shows in his sobering *Surveillance in the Time of Insecurity* that several different kinds of 'security cultures' and their corresponding 'surveillance infrastructures' have similar consequences of engendering insecurities, along with aggravating social inequalities. In the United States, from which most of his examples come, Monahan says that 'a unifying thread is fear of the Other'.[66] The added twist, in Monahan's account, is that to cope with every fresh fear, every new insecurity, ordinary citizens are encouraged to do two things: one, shoulder the burden by stockpiling supplies, installing alarms or buying insurance; and two, endorse extreme measures, including torture and domestic spying.

With all this in view, it seems to me that using a term like 'liquid surveillance' is once again warranted. This is the kind of surveillance suited to liquid times and bearing some of the tell-tale signs of contemporary liquidity. We fall over ourselves trying to make life-with-fear liveable, but each attempt produces more risks, more fears. The horrors of 9/11 and its aftermath are symptomatic of this, but only symptomatic. Categorized innocents are now at risk and in fear in an ironic parody of terrorism. And the problem is far more general than what happens in airport security and at border checkpoints. So may we start this segment by commenting on the premodern to modern and then the liquid modern shifts in security-prompted surveillance? What has really changed and are some features of premodern security surveillance – hinted at in my biblical and Shakespearean examples – permanently lost?

Zygmunt Bauman   Once more we are in full agreement . . .

First, Francisco, with or without the benefits of modern electronics, guarded the security of Elsinore castle against the dangers oozing from '*outside* the city' – that poorly controlled vast space populated by brigands, highway robbers and other sorts of unnamed yet menacing unknowns. His successors guard the city against uncountable menaces lurking *inside* the city, gestated inside the city. The urban citadels of security have turned through the centuries into greenhouses or incubators of genuine or putative, endemic or contrived dangers. Built with the idea of cutting out islands of order from a sea of chaos, cities have turned into the most profuse fountains of disorder, calling for visible and invisible walls, barricades, watchtowers and embrasures – and innumerable armed men.

Second, as you point out, quoting Monahan, 'the unifying thread' of all those inner-city security contraptions 'is fear of the Other'. But that 'Other' we tend to, or are nudged to be afraid of is not some individual or some category of individuals who have put themselves, or have been forced, beyond the bounds of the city and denied the right of settlement or sojourn. Rather, that Other is a neighbour, passer-by, loiterer, stalker: ultimately, every stranger. But then, as we all know, city-dwellers are strangers to each other, and we are all suspected of carrying danger, and so we all to one degree or another want the floating, diffuse and unnamed threats to be condensed and congested into a set of 'usual suspects'. This condensation is hoped to keep the menace at a distance, and also, simultaneously, to protect us from the danger of being classified as part of the menace.

It is for that double reason – to be protected from the dangers *and* from being cast into the class of a danger – that we develop vested interests in a dense network of surveilling, selecting, separating and excluding measures. We all need to mark the enemies of security in order to *avoid being counted among them* . . . We need to accuse in order to be absolved; to exclude in order to avoid exclusion. We need to trust in the efficacy of surveillance devices to give us the comfort of believing that we, decent creatures that we are, will escape unscathed from the ambushes such devices set – and will thereby be reinstated and reconfirmed in our decency and in the propriety of our ways. A curious and fateful shift indeed in the meaning of John Donne's centuries-old message: 'No man is an island, entire of itself; every man is a piece of the Continent, a part of the main . . . And therefore never send to know for whom the bell tolls; it tolls for thee'. . .

And third, by now, it seems, we all, or at least the great majority of us, have turned into security addicts. Having ingested and assimilated the *Weltanschauung* of the ubiquity of danger, of the comprehensiveness of the grounds for mistrust and suspicion, of the notion of safe cohabitation as conceivable solely as an artefact of continuous vigilance, we have become dependent on surveillance being done and being seen to be done. As Anna Minton observes, 'the need for security can become addictive, with people finding that however much they have it can never be enough and that rather like an addictive drug, once they have got used to it they can't do without it'.[67] 'Fear breeds fear', so Minton concludes, and I fully agree; I believe you do as well. Singular, lonely resistance against the general trend and well-nigh universal mood is of little use; it calls for a strong will and it is socially and financially expensive. Elaine, for instance, one of Anna Minton's cases, was surprised after moving home by 'the sheer amount of security already there – from CCTV to numerous locks and double locks on the doors and windows and multiple, highly complex alarm systems'. Elaine felt uncomfortable in an environment that constantly reminded her of the need to feel afraid, to look fearfully around and take precautions, and so she wanted most of those contraptions removed. 'But that was easier said than done. When she finally managed to find builders to take the locks away, they were amazed at what she wanted and told her they rarely found themselves on that sort of job.'

By the way, Agnes Heller noted in a recent issue of the *Thesis Eleven* quarterly a symptomatic shift in contemporary historical novels. Unlike their predecessors, authors locating their plots in bygone, premodern times hardly ever focus on outrages perpetrated by foreign armies, invasions or wars, even if there was clearly no shortage of these in the times in which their stories are set. Instead, they focus on the 'ambient fear' permeating daily life – of being charged with witchcraft, heresy, theft or murder . . . Authors born and bred in our times impute retrospectively to our ancestors and read into their motives the kinds of horrors typical of our own security obsessed and addicted era. The sources of nightmares have moved in their world map, so to speak, from 'out there' to 'in here'. They spring up in the nearest coffee houses or pubs, among the next door neighbours – and sometimes they even settle in our own kitchen or bedroom.

This is the paradox of the world saturated with surveillance devices, whatever their ostensible purpose: on the one hand, we are more protected from insecurity than any past generation; on the other hand, though, no previous, pre-electronic generation found the feelings of insecurity such a daily (and nightly) experience . . .

DL I couldn't agree with you more, Zygmunt. But I want to press you on one or two points. Let's start with those 'feelings of insecurity'. They exist at many levels and contribute, not to a generalized 'culture of fear' as some have suggested, but to multiple cultures of fear. At one level, for instance, there are the fears associated with being part of a proscribed minority, a risky Muslim Arab in the West. A few weeks ago I met Maher Arar for the first time; he is a Canadian engineer who, through a series of egregious errors by Canadian security agencies and then a peremptory apprehension by US authorities in New York, ended up as a torture victim in Syria in 2002–3. Extraordinary rendition, based on a mishandling of highly dubious data, threatened to destroy his health, his family life, indeed everything he naturally held dear. But the insecurities of so-called risk societies not only affect people like Arar with no demonstrable connection with terrorism (including those who do not even have 'Middle Eastern' traits), but also people warned that genetic tests indicate their proclivity to certain diseases, or parents anxious to protect their offspring from downtown dangers . . .

What these cases have in common is that security is seen as something relating to a majority, leaving the abnormal, the statistical deviations, at the margins. So Arab Muslims in the West, but also the minority whose genes supposedly point to possible disease or those vulnerable to night-time street risks, are all touched by insecurity. Security's imagined future is one in which all abnormalities (terrorism, disease, violence) have been excluded or at least contained. And as Didier Bigo says, surveillance actually connects what Foucault split apart – discipline and security – such that in a sense security *is* surveillance as its ever evolving techniques monitor mobilities in a risk-ridden world.[68] Insecurities are a practical corollary of today's securitized societies.

Thus we can say that the technologies of in/security cannot be understood merely as products of information and communication technologies, or even as the result of our being trapped in states of exception (galvanized but not initiated by 9/11). Rather, they are part of a larger social and political configuration, relating to risk and its close cousin, uncertainty. So how do we approach it, politically? With many others who have not succumbed to cynicism about the possibility that we could 'make a difference', I would like to think that there are strategies for questioning and pushing back against these developments that turn in/security into such critical categories for life chances. Yet if I understand you right, then power and politics are increasingly drifting apart in liquid times, so that the former is evaporating into Manuel Castells' 'space of flows', leaving politics languishing in the space of places.[69]

This notion is persuasive but in a sense paralysing because it implies that only a global politics – which does not yet exist – could have any real effect. I agree with you that pursuing the commensurability of power and politics is a worthy goal, but what of the chances of a politics in which democracy (and thus account-ability) and liberty (that is so sorely circumscribed by the security–surveillance alliance) could be the focus of struggle at more local levels?

ZB Houellebecq – a writer whom I much admire for his perspicacity and his uncanny knack of spying out the general in the particular, as well as for extrapolat-ing and unravelling its inner potential, and the author of *The Possibility of an Island*, the most insightful dystopia thus far of our deregulated, fragmented and individualized, liquid modern society – could be some-one you have in mind when you single out those who have 'succumbed to cynicism about the possibility that we could make a difference'. He is very sceptical and unhopeful, and he piles up valid reasons to remain that way. I am not in full agreement with his stance, but I don't find it easy to refute his reasons . . .

The authors of the greatest dystopias of yore, like Zamyatin, Orwell or Aldous Huxley, penned their visions of the horrors haunting the denizens of the solid modern world: the closely regimented and order-obsessed world of producers and soldiers. Set on red alert, those authors hoped that their visions would shock their fellow travellers into the unknown into shaking off the torpor of sheep marching meekly to the slaughterhouse: this is the sort of world into which your self-inflicted equanimity is bound to usher you, they said – unless you rebel. Zamyatin, Orwell, Huxley, just like Houellebecq, were children of their times. This is why, *unlike* Houellebecq, they believed in bespoke tailors: in commissioning the future to order, and dismissing as a gross incongruity the idea of a self-made future. What they were frightened of were wrong measurements, unshapely designs and/or sloppy, drunk or corrupt tailors; they had no fear, though, that tailors' shops would go bankrupt and fall apart, be decommissioned or phased out – and they did not anticipate the advent of a world squeezed empty of bespoke tailors.

Houellebecq, however, writes from the innards of just such a tailor-free world. The future, in such a world, is *self*-made: a DIY future, which none of the DIY addicts controls, wishes to control, or could control. Once each is set on his or her own, never criss-crossing orbit, the contemporaries of Houellebecq no longer need dispatchers or conductors, any more than the planets and stars need road planners and traffic monitors. They are perfectly capable of finding the road to the slaughterhouse on their own. And they do – like the two principal protagonists of Houellebecq's story, hoping (in vain, alas, in vain . . .) to meet each other on that road. The slaughterhouse in Houellebecq's dystopia is also, as it were, DIY.

In an interview conducted by Susannah Hunnewell,[70] Houellebecq does not beat about the bush – and just as his predecessors did, and as we do and our ancestors did, he recasts into a programme of his choice conditions not of his choice: 'What I think, fundamentally, is that you can't do anything about major societal changes.' Following the same thinking, he points out a few sentences later that even if he regrets what is currently happening in the world, he doesn't 'have any interest in turning back the clock *because* I don't believe it can be done' (emphasis added). If Houellebecq's predecessors were concerned about what the agents at the command post of 'major societal changes' might do to stifle the irritating randomness of individual behaviour, Houellebecq's concern is about where that randomness of individual behaviour will lead in the absence of command posts and the agents willing to man them with 'major societal change' in mind. It is not the *excess* of control and of coercion – its loyal and inseparable companion – that worries Houellebecq; it is their *dearth* that renders all worry toothless and superfluous. Houellebecq reports from an aircraft whose pilot's cabin is empty.

'I don't believe much in the influence of politics on history . . . I also don't believe that individual psychology has any effect on social movements' – Houellebecq concludes. In other words, the question of 'what is to be done' is invalidated and pre-empted by the emphatic answer of 'no one' to the question of 'who is going to do it'. The sole agents in sight are 'technological factors and sometimes, not often, religious'. But technology is notorious for its blindness; it reverses the human sequence of actions following purposes (the very sequence that sets the agent apart from other moving bodies) – it moves because it can move (or because it can't stand still), not because it wants to arrive; while God, in addition to an inscrutability that dazzles and blinds his watchers, stands for the failings of humans and their inadequacy to the task (that is, for their inability to face up to the odds and act effectively on their intentions). The impotent are guided by the blind; being impotent, they have no other choice. Not, at any rate, if they are abandoned to their own, jarringly and abominably inadequate resources; not without a pilot with eyes wide open – a pilot looking *and* seeing. 'Technological' and 'religious' factors behave uncannily like Nature: no one can really be sure where they are going to land until they land there; but that only means, as Houellebecq would put it, until the clock can no longer be turned back.

Houellebecq, with his praiseworthy self-awareness and frankness, puts on record the vanity of hope, in case someone is sufficiently stubborn and naive to go on entertaining hope. Describing things, he insists, no longer leads to changing them; forecasting what is going to happen no longer leads to preventing it from happening. Has a point of no return finally been reached? Has Fukuyama's verdict been vindicated, even while its grounds are refuted and ridiculed?

I question Houellebecq's verdict, even though I am in almost full agreement with his inventory of its grounds and likelihood. Almost – because that inventory contains the truth, only the truth, but not the whole truth. Something tremendously important has been left out of Houellebecq's account: it is because the weaknesses of politicians and of individual psychology are *not the only* things to blame for the bleakness of the (correctly!) painted prospects that the point we have been brought to thus far *is not* a point of no return. But you are surely aware of the likely source of both my approval and my reservations, since you point to the looming divorce between power (the ability to do things) and politics (the ability to select things to be done).

Indeed, Houellebecq's despondency and defeatism derive from the two-tier crisis of agency. On the upper tier, at the level of the nation-state, agency has been brought perilously close to impotence, and that is because power, once locked in a tight embrace with state politics, is now evaporating into the global, extraterritorial 'space of flows', far beyond the reach of the persistently territorial politics of the state. State institutions are now burdened with the task of inventing and providing local solutions to globally produced problems; due to a shortage of power, this is a load the state cannot carry and a task it cannot perform with its remaining resources and within the shrinking realm of its feasible options. The desperate yet widespread response to that antinomy is the tendency to shed, one by one, the numerous functions the modern state was expected to and did perform, even though with mixed success – while still resting its legitimation on the promise of their continued performance. The functions successively abandoned or forfeited are shed to the lower tier – the sphere of 'life politics', the area where individuals are nominated to the dubious office of their own legislative, executive and judicial authorities rolled into one. It is now the 'individuals by decree' who are expected to devise and pursue, with the skills and resources they individually possess, their individual solutions to the societally generated problems (this, in a nutshell, is the meaning of the 'individualization' of the present day, a process in which the deepening of dependency is disguised as and redubbed the progress of autonomy). As on the upper tier, on the lower one the tasks are grossly mismatched with the available and attainable means to perform them. Hence the feeling of haplessness, of impotence: the plankton-like experience of having been a priori, irreparably and irreversibly condemned to defeat in a blatantly unequal confrontation with overwhelmingly vehement tides.

The yawning gap between the grandiosity of the pressures and the meagreness of the defences is bound to go on feeding and beefing up the sentiments of impotence as long as it persists. That gap, however, is *not* bound to persist: the gap looks unbridgeable only when the future is depicted as 'more of the same', an extrapolation of present trends – and the belief that the point of no return has already been reached adds credibility to this extrapolation without necessarily rendering it correct. Dystopias do, as it happens, turn time and again into self-refuting prophesies, as the fate of Zamyatin's and Orwell's visions at least suggests . . .

DL Thank you for being so candid yourself, Zygmunt. I'm struck by the fact that this takes us right back to our earliest discussions (in the 1980s) about the utopian and dystopian. Each literary genre opens possibilities for seeing beyond the present: the one strains to view a promised land that is just plausible enough to be worth working for but that simultaneously stretches the imagination towards hitherto unknown features of human sociality, while the other extrapolates from the most anxiety-generating and socially destructive tendencies of the day to show how we'll soon be shut permanently into a pathetic and punishing prospect. The growth of computer-assisted surveillance as a dimension of security-obsessed *il*liberal democracies has certainly fuelled recent dystopian – and sometimes despairing – imaginations. This is seen to varying extents in movies such as *Brazil* (1985), *Bladerunner* (1992), *Gattaca* (1997), *Minority Report* (2002), as well as in the persuasive proposal of legal scholar Daniel Solove that Kafka offers more appropriate metaphors than Orwell for today's surveillance.[71]

On the other hand, a wariness of overwatched futures does not yet seem to have stemmed the flood of futurism (I hesitate to dignify it with the term 'utopianism') and digital dreaming. The notion of cyberspace certainly caught on as what Vincent Mosco calls a 'mythic space' that transcends ordinary worlds of time, space and politics; he calls it the 'digital sublime'.[72] Ever since the invention of the silicon chip in 1978, technological utopians have gushed about 'microelectronics revolutions' and 'information societies', and iconic info-age entrepreneurs like Steve Jobs achieved supercelebrity status. Plenty of pundits still seem to think that the best-of-all-possible-worlds is digital; this goes for democracy, organization, entertainment and of course for security and military engagement. Within these, of course, surveillance is prominent. As American Major S. F. Murray says, for instance, contemporary battle command begins with 'one's ability to see, visualize, observe or find'.[73]

But in your work we find an entirely different depth to what might still be called utopian thought which I think immediately exposes the shallowness of digital dreams. I checked what I recalled from your book on *Socialism: The Active Utopia*, where you observe that people climb

> successive hills only to discover from their tops virgin territories which their never-appeased spirit of transcendence urges them to explore. Beyond each successive hill they

hope to find the peacefulness of the end. What they do find is the excitement of the beginning. Today as two thousand years ago, 'hope that is seen is not hope. For who hopes for what he sees?' (Paul to the Romans 8: 24).[74]

I'm definitely with you on the 'never-appeased spirit of transcendence' but I also wonder if the 'beginning' and the 'end' of which you speak – or perhaps of which Paul speaks – might have more in common than we allow. That the peacefulness inscribed in the original might be fulfilled in the future . . .

Wherever that thought leads, I assume from what you say that the utopian and dystopian muses still offer scope for imaginative critiques, including those that set their sights on information and surveillance. Keith Tester's take on your stance resonates with me when he says that your 'utopianism signifies the praxis of possibility that seeks critically to open up the world against the ossification of actuality by common sense, alienation and brute power'.[75] What I find refreshing in your work is that you show 'that the world doesn't have to be the way it is and that there is an alternative to what presently seems so natural, so obvious, so inevitable'.[76] At the World Social Forum in Mumbai a few years ago I was blown away by the thousands of people from many different countries who were also inspired by the slogan 'Other worlds are possible . . . '

With regard to surveillance in its guise as security's handmaiden, this does indeed offer insight. Unblinking electronic eyes on the street, comprehensive data harvesting, the increasingly high-pressure flows of personal information are each viewed as rational responses to rife risks. We desperately need to hear voices asking why? what for? and, have you any idea what the human consequences are of all this? I listen hard, hoping to hear someone say, 'could there be other ways of conceiving what's wrong with the world and how its ills might be addressed?'

ZB If you allow me, I would dearly wish us to dare just one step further – but in my view an important step; indeed, the ultimate step that may well take us to the deepest, perpetually billowing and inexhaustible source of our restlessness, of which the desire for more and more surveillance is but one manifestation, though arguably one of the most spectacular as well as most thought provoking. Namely, the hub of the human, all-too-human and inherent urge for transcendence is the drive towards comfort and convenience; to a habitat that is neither worrisome nor wearisome, that is fully transparent, holding no surprises and mysteries, never taking us aback or catching us unprepared; a world with no contingency or accidents, 'unanticipated consequences' or reverses of fate. Such an ultimate peace of body and mind is, I suspect, the essence of the popular, intuitive idea of 'order'; it lurks underneath every and any variety of the bustle to make order and maintain it, starting from a housewife (or househusband) busily keeping bathroom things in the bathroom and kitchen things in the kitchen, bedroom things in the bedroom and drawing room things in the drawing room, and stretching all the way to the gatekeepers – receptionists and security guards separating those with the right of entry from those destined to stay stuck elsewhere, and all in all struggling to create a space in which nothing moves unless it is moved. As I am sure you've noted, the place most closely approximating that vision of the end of anxieties about contingency is the graveyard – the fullest and most comprehensive incarnation of the intuition of 'order' . . .

Freud would say that the restlessness we express by fixing ever more locks and TV cameras on doors and passages is guided by Thanatos, the death instinct! Paradoxically, we are restless because of our insatiable desire for rest, never to be fully gratified as long as we stay alive. That desire inspired and instilled by Thanatos can, after all, be met only in death; the irony, though, is that this vision of a 'final order' shaped like a graveyard is precisely what makes us compulsive, obsessive and addictive 'order builders' and thereby keeps us alive, listless, perpetually anxious and prompted to transcend today what we managed to arrive at yesterday. It is the unquenched and insatiable thirst for order that makes us experience each reality as disorderly and calling out for reform. I guess surveillance is one of the very few industries never needing to fear running out of steam and working itself out of a job . . .

DL Of course we can push the edge of our conversation towards issues of transcendence, to an inquiry about the roots of the desire for peace of body and mind, and even to querying whether or not the apparently insatiable appetite for surveillance ironically springs from the death instinct. These questions certainly take us well beyond the security-surveillance-industrial complex while also supplying potential clues as to why such an enterprise might be blooming while others wilt.

For myself, I have no reason not to nod in agreement with you that visions of a 'final order' may well lie half-hidden behind contemporary obsessions with security, or that desires for 'rest' relate in significant ways to our human restlessness, although I confess that I'm less sure that such visions are 'shaped like a grave-yard'. (This despite the fact that our home overlooks a park that was previously a cemetery, divided neatly in 1816 into 'Scots, Irish and English' sections, cor-responding with who would officiate over burials, the Presbyterians, Catholics or Anglicans. It also contained a separate section for those too poor to be included in one of the others. The historical sociology of burial grounds is illuminating.)

However, perhaps you will let me comment on how I would approach the issue of security and surveillance on this broad canvas (and maybe leave the question of the canvas itself for a later conversation)? Although 9/11 did not in itself produce that obsession with secu-rity, it did much to promote the security-surveillance boom that has both provided a major profit boost for related industries and also succeeded in reproduc-ing intensified everyday surveillance regimes in urban areas throughout the global north, and especially in the United States. Here is a particular instance of the 'sublime', as I mentioned earlier. 'Homeland Security' statements are hymns to 'transcendence through tech-nology', about which David Noble and Vincent Mosco write so eloquently.[77] Such great faith is vested in each new technology that, importantly, questioning them may be viewed as sacrilege or blasphemy.

One probably has to go back to the Renaissance to find the proximate roots of the idea that peace and prosperity can be engineered through science and technology, a conviction that was bolstered by much

Enlightenment thinking.[78] While the Renaissance was in part an understandable reaction against the medieval authoritarian church in Europe, the notion of contriving to bring about the reign of peace and prosperity through the mechanism of invention precisely reversed a long-held belief that – as you yourself have quoted – if you want peace, seek justice. In the Jewish Torah, doing justice and loving one's neighbour is the route to peace (or *shalom*, signalling wholeness, integrity and the right relationships all round between God, creation and human beings). The Christian equivalent would be Jesus' 'seek first the kingdom of God and all these things will be added'.

So I see this commitment to the efficacy of technique and invention – today's science and technology – to procure peace in terms of a false quest for an impossible guarantee of security. The belief that bigger, faster, more connected technologies of surveillance in the service of security can somehow guarantee peace is palpably mistaken and, fatefully, closes off other options. In a response to the snowballing surveillance after 9/11 I commented:

> Jacques Ellul once noted, reflecting on the fate of ancient cities such as Babylon and Nineveh, that these cultures were closed, too, 'protected against attacks from the outside, in a security built up in walls and machines'. Is there anything new under the sun? Yet against that, insists Ellul, is the vision of a city where doing justice and loving one's neighbour is put first. From that commitment to responsibility for the Other proceeds peace and prosperity, freedom and security, sought otherwise through false priorities. This is a city whose gates are never shut. It is a place of inclusion

and trust. And its light finally banishes all that is now done in the dark.[79]

My comments followed an analysis of post-9/11 surveillance developments that highlighted their tendency to tighten exclusion (the ban-opticon), to foster fear and to shroud decision-making in a veil of secrecy.

5

Consumerism, new media and social sorting

David Lyon   A central theme of your work, Zygmunt, has been to expose the ways in which consumerism has grown so central to the production of social divisions but also to identities. I was among those who welcomed *Work, Consumerism and the New Poor* when it first appeared in 1998. But a paradox here, as I see it, is that while consumption entails the pleasurable seduction of consumers, this seduction is also the result of systematic surveillance on a massive scale. If this was not obvious through previous forms of database marketing, the advent of Amazon, Facebook and Google indicates the current state of the art. Yet Thomas Mathiesen, in the preface to a recent book on *Internet and Surveillance*, also points out how hidden this is: 'Below the surface there is an enormous hinterland of undiscovered surveillance practices based on use of the internet . . . the vast trail of electronic signs that we leave behind as we go about our daily affairs – in banks, shops, trade centres, and everywhere else, every day of the year.'[80]

As we turn from considering the urgent matters

relating to security and surveillance towards the question of consumption it may seem that we can breathe more freely. After all, this is the realm of fun, of the flâneur, of freedom. Think again! Here we find detailed management operating, based once again on gathering personal data on a huge scale, for concatenation, classification and for treating different categories of consumers differently, based on their profile. Consider what a boon it is to many that Amazon.com, through its techniques of 'collaborative filtering', can tell us what books others buy, similar to the one whose purchase we're contemplating. Every transaction generates information about itself that is then used to guide further consumer choices. A few years ago I combined your ideas on the wooing of consumers with those of Gary T. Marx on police classifications of likely suspects ('categorical suspicion') to create the hybrid concept of 'categorical seduction'.[81] I still think it works.

Amazon.com, however, also cheerfully makes consumers aware of how they are surveilled by others, through their Wish List feature.[82] It isn't entirely a hidden process! So far from being secretive, this feature can in principle be checked by anyone. The Wish List also reminds us of how much people *like* to be watched; there is a kind of shoppers' scopophilia working here.[83] As danah boyd points out, the voyeur meets the fl âneur courtesy of social media.[84] But not only this, the Wish List gives consumers the opportunity to manage themselves, to show a particular face to others. Amazon.com succeeds, it seems, in managing customers through their ongoing relationship and also through offering the chance to indulge in a little impression management on the side.

At the end of the day, however, Amazon.com acquires the data it needs, leaving its customers happily inhabiting what Eli Pariser tellingly calls their 'filter bubble'.[85] It is fairly well known that different people Googling with the same word come up with different results. This is because Google refines its search results according to your previous queries. Likewise, those with many Facebook friends will only receive updates from those that Facebook thinks they wish to hear about, on the basis of the frequency of their interaction with those people. Amazon.com fits this model too of course. Pariser's parallel, and justifiable, concern is that 'personalization filters serve up a kind of invisible autopropaganda, indoctrinating us with our own ideas, amplifying our desire for things that are familiar and leaving us oblivious to the dangers lurking in the dark territory of the unknown'.

But the broader backdrop is that the overall effects of consumer surveillance, especially through all kinds of internet use, are not only to cream off those contented consumers and promise further rewards and benefits, but also to cut off those who don't conform to expectations. I mentioned earlier Oscar Gandy's work on this, which shows how, in several domains, the 'rational discrimination' carried out by corporations has negative effects for some. As Gandy states,

> The statistical discrimination enabled by sophisticated analytics contributes to the cumulative disadvantage that weighs down, isolates, excludes, and ultimately widens the gaps between those at the top, and nearly everyone else. Although observers have tended to focus on the use of these systems in support of targeted advertising online,

their reach is far more extensive. It covers access to a range of goods and services, including markets for finance and housing, as well as health care, education, and social services.[86]

These are all themes that illustrate 'liquid surveillance', now in a consumer mode, and I'm sure you'd like to comment on more than one of them! But can we start the ball rolling with a query that comes from your own work? It seems to me that your concern with the exclusionary effects of surveillance – with which I heartily concur – sometimes leads you to minimize the ways that the same liquid surveillant mechanisms exert pressure on *all* consumers. True, if one believes that social analysis should have particular concerns for those who are marginalized and shut out, understanding the mechanisms that facilitate this is vital. But the same surveillant power produces a variety of behaviours, affecting different groups differently. Surely it is in part through the normalizing of the majority, in this case through categorical seduction, that the minority become subject to cumulative disadvantage?

Zygmunt Bauman A few decades ago the great upheaval (or great leap forward, as recorded in the annals of marketing art) in the progress of consumerist society was the passage from needs satisfaction (that is, from production targeted at existing demand) to needs creation (that is, to demand targeted at existing production) – through tempting, seducing and beefing up the desire so aroused. That strategic shift brought an enormous advance in results, coupled, however, with a considerable rise in their cost: 'creating demand' (read,

arousing and sustaining the desire to obtain and possess) calls for continuously high expenditure. Costs are
in principle non-reducible: each new product thrown on
to the market requires desire to be conjured up virtually
from scratch, as desires are always targeted and specific,
and therefore non-transferable.

We are currently going through the third segment of
the Hegelian triad. Given the generally well-entrenched
propensity to seek satisfaction in the commodities on
offer and the universal readiness to identify 'new' with
'improved' – as well as the sophistication of the technology of record-keeping which allows that readiness
to be located when it is at its most 'ripe' to respond
promptly to the enticement – another seminal shift can
be accomplished: towards targeting offers at persons or
categories of persons already mellowed to enthusiastically accept them. The most costly part of the previous
marketing strategy – the *arousing* of desires – is thereby
written out of the marketing budget and transferred on
to the shoulders of prospective consumers. As in the
case of surveillance, the marketing of goods becomes
more and more a DIY job, and the resulting servitude
becomes more and more voluntary . . . Whenever I enter
Amazon's site, I am now greeted with a series of titles
'selected especially for you, Zygmunt'. Given the record
of my past book purchases, the high probability is that
I'll be tempted . . . And as a rule I am! Obviously, thanks
to my dutiful, even if inadvertent, cooperation, the
Amazon servers now know my preferences or hobbies
better than I do. No longer do I consider their suggestions to be commercials; I view them as friendly help
in facilitating my progress through the book-market
jungle. And I am grateful. And with every new purchase

I pay to update my preferences in their database and unerringly direct my future purchases . . .

Targeting the ready-to-use niches of the market, a way to proceed that calls for no preliminary investment of means but promises instant results, is an area exceptionally suited to the deployment of surveillance technology – as if made to its measure; it is on that new frontline that the most rapid and remarkable progress in surveillance technology has been recently recorded, and where yet more rapid and remarkable growth can be expected in the foreseeable future. The example of Amazon which you so aptly discuss is indeed trail-blazing; opening, let me repeat, into the last segment of the Hegelian triad in its application in the history of marketing. Other companies have followed suit after Amazon, and many more are lining up to join in. The tools of marketing surveillance get sharpened and further adjusted in the process of their diffusion. In the marketing practised on Facebook, for instance, potentially off-putting references to the personal predilections of the recipient of the offer are not made; 'socially correct' references, inoffensive to the partisans of personal freedoms, are made instead – references to the likes and preferences and favourite acquisitions of one's friends. Indeed, an intentionally and unashamedly restrictive, panopticon-style undertaking is disguised as an instance of the benevolently hospitable, socially friendly synopticon run under the banner of solidarity . . .

All that targeting, of course, only applies to fully fledged, fully feathered consumers. Its application to flawed or indolent consumers, the 'usual suspects' which ban-opticons are designed to spot, pinpoint and excise, would be a sheer waste of resources. In the area of consumerist surveillance, panoptic and synoptic appliances are set into operation once the ground-cleansing job of ban-opticons has been completed.

DL Yes, exactly. And this is another reason why I think that your 'liquid modernity' theorem is so suited to studying surveillance. Where consumerism reigns, so-called social media are rather limitedly *social*;[87] as you say, they could be read as a synopticon under the seductively situated solidarity banner. Liquid modern consumers, egged on by electronic devices, tend to be turned in on themselves as pleasure-seeking individuals. Indeed, I once heard an undergraduate student complain (in a curious juxtaposition of discourses) that 'we have a right to have fun'. The filter bubbles offered by social media but inflated by us as we blow our preferences and predilections into them with every click of the mouse simply reproduce that liquid modern, consumerist 'introversion' that is simultaneously and paradoxically a form of extroversion, a desire for publicness.

As I see it, this relates to a long-term process in Western cultures, where scopophilia (or the love of being seen) merges with the growing ubiquity of surveillance practices, with several striking effects. One concerns the rather obvious willing involvement of consumers in their own surveillance. As we were saying, with the Amazon example, we can fully understand, from within as it were, the attraction of this process. But I strongly suspect that this phenomenon, which could equally but more critically be read as carelessness with one's personal information, may also lull us into greater complacency about the travels of our digital personas. Rather than asking why the person behind the counter requires our telephone number, driver's licence and postal code, or querying the machine-demand for more data before the transaction can be completed, we assume that there must be a reason that will benefit us. For instance, when it comes to the, now widespread, use of 'loyalty cards' from chain stores, airlines and the like, a recent international study shows that people 'either don't know or don't care' about the connections between the use of loyalty cards and profiling.[88]

Beyond this, however, the filter bubbles that increasingly try to turn our market category into a niche of one consumer also facilitate ignorance about others who may have been filtered right out by the same triage. If people 'don't know or don't care' about the online profiling of consumers, it doesn't take much imagination to infer that they are likely to be even less knowledgeable about the consumer ban-opticon, with its rather brutally termed 'demarketing' of failed consumers. Not to mention the other ban-opticons that lurk in urban spaces, such as those cutting off proscribed populations from essential services on the basis of their personal profiles, or those valorizing some city districts while demonizing others – which connects back to a previous conversation. As Stephen Graham shows, certain American cities, as well as ones in faraway Afghanistan and elsewhere, have become 'battlespaces' and thus targets, also based on population profiles.[89] And here the military and the market work together, in what James Der Derian calls the 'military-industrial-media-entertainment complex'.[90]

In all these ways and more, then, it seems that the comfort-centred worlds of consumer surveillance evidence curious connections with the more familiar faces of surveillance. They are mutually supporting, mutually augmenting . . .[91]

ZB Technology is indeed transferable – and keenly transferred in this case, just as in a multitude of other cases. It would not be easy, I guess, to decide which sector of the new (widened, and so presumably yet more formidable) 'complex' plays the pioneering role; until relatively recently – during the Cold War and subsequent military adventures of the aspiring, yet ultimately failed world empire – the most common opinion believed the military to be in the lead. It seems, though, that the continuing centrality of public security in declared state policies is nowadays sustained more by the state's legitimation concerns than by the 'facts of the matter' – those facts shifting the centre of gravity towards the commercial (including the 'media-entertainment') sector of the 'complex'.

You surely know more about the current state of affairs in this area than I do, but I'd surmise that the R&D departments of big commercial companies are in the process of taking over the lead in the present-day development of surveillance gadgets and strategies from the top-secret military laboratories. I do not have the statistics – I count here on you being in a better position, having studied the matter much more deeply than I have – but I surmise that nowadays it is not only that the truly big money tends to drift there, but also that in times of economic depression those R&D departments belong to the very few areas that are still 'cuts free' and immune to cuts in the otherwise truncated or severely trimmed body of venture capital.

As to the silent or vociferous, conscious or

inadvertent, intentional or by default, but undoubtedly massive cooperation of the surveilled in the business of surveillance bent on their 'profiling', I would not ascribe it (at least not primarily) to the '*love* of being seen'. Hegel famously defined freedom as necessity learned and recognized . . . The passion for putting oneself on record is a foremost, perhaps the most blatant example of that Hegelian rule in our times in which the updated and adjusted version of Descartes' cogito is 'I am seen (watched, noted, recorded) therefore I am'.

The arrival of the internet has put within the grasp of every Tom, Dick and Harry a feat that once required night escapades by a few trained and adventurous graffiti artists: making the invisible visible, rendering the neglected, ignored and abandoned blatantly, jarringly present – in short, making one's being-in-the-world tangible and irrefutable. Or, to recall the diagnosis made dozens of years ago by Dick Hebdige of the Birmingham Centre for Contemporary Cultural Studies, it has come to replace the job of lifting oneself out of invisibility and oblivion, and so claiming a foothold in an admittedly alien and inhospitable world, by breaking bottles or necks . . . Seen against this background, gaining being-in-the-world with the help of Facebook carries an advantage over daubing graffiti, calling for no hard-to-acquire skills and being 'risk-free' (no police breathing down your neck), legal, widely recognized, acknowledged and respected. The urge is much the same; it is the means of channelling it that improve and grow in availability and ease of handling . . . Surrendering to necessity turns into fun?

The urge in question, still as massive and overwhelming, if not more so, as in the pre-internet era, arises from the widespread sense of having been abandoned and neglected, forced into invisibility amidst the bazaar of colourful and seductive images; it generates sentiments that, to use a recent suggestion by *Le Monde*, 'oscillate between numb anger and resentful desperation'. I believe that in the last account it is that urge and those sentiments that bear most of the responsibility for the enormous, astonishing success of the activity of 'DIY profiling'.

6

Probing surveillance ethically

David Lyon Each theme of our conversation thus far raises questions not only about the appropriate analysis of surveillance – is it liquid? what difference does this make? – but also about the insistent ethical challenges accompanying, or rather, built into, formative of, such analysis. One of the best-known academic whistleblowers on today's surveillance, Gary Marx, urged back in 1998 that ethics was needed for the 'new surveillance'.[92] Largely because it's one of the very few 'ethical' pieces in the field, it tends to be quoted because at least he tries to make some headway in this area. He argues that technological change happens so rapidly and with such profound consequences in the surveillance field that older forms of regulation badly need updating.

In other words, Marx's laudable work offers guidance for legal and regulatory intervention in relation to the spread of surveillance. He puts a priority on the dignity of persons and emphasizes the avoidance of harms, whether or not people are aware that they are under surveillance, and other broad principles suited for translation into rules. As I say, Marx's studies of surveillance have been definitive for the developing field. He was one of the first, for example, to insist that what he called *categorical* suspicion has to be considered alongside more conventional, individual kinds when software and statistics help to determine who is of interest to the police.[93]

Although Marx's ethical principles are broad ones, they do have the virtue of speaking to specific situations, in the hope that alternative practices can be forged. But for myself, I have a nagging feeling that there are ethical issues that we also need to confront on quite another plane. Without wanting the discussion to levitate into a realm disconnected from the 'harms' and hurts associated with new surveillance techniques – of which we've had a fair bit to say in our discussion – it seems to me that some fundamental ethical issues confront us as technologically mediated surveillance envelops our lives on a day-to-day basis.

May we step back for a moment? It is clear that some of the earliest dreams of 'cybernetics' (from the 1950s) have come home to roost in 'cyberspace' and its sidekick, surveillance. The sorts of control through feedback loops that were sought after for industrial manufacturing purposes and that migrated to general administration before being generalized as the basic strategy of organizational practice in the twenty-first century are central to what I have in mind. Not for nothing do authors as far apart as Gilles Deleuze and David Garland see burgeoning surveillance in relation to, respectively, 'societies of control' and 'cultures of control'.[94] And while today the control has largely liquefied, as opposed to operating in the fixed spaces and enclosures of the panopticon, the old motif beloved of Bentham is still visible (or may be made visible by people brave enough to disclose and expose it).

Part of the story here is, as Katherine Hayles poignantly puts it, how information lost its body.[95] The cybernetics that budded in the 1950s was not unconnected with the emerging definition of information that, to put it briefly, conceived of information as something quantifiable and commodifiable. In the postwar years, communication theorists engaged in a transatlantic series of 'summit' meetings, known as the Macy conferences, to thrash out how information would be conceived in this rapidly expanding field. The British participant in those fateful meetings, neuroscientist Donald MacKay of Keele University, contended in vain that information, to count as such, had to have a demonstrable association with meaning. But the so-called American School – Claude Shannon in particular – won the day, with the result that 'information' would increasingly be used in communication theory as an entity cut loose from its human and meaning*ful* origins.

Let's moor this in today's surveillance realities. More and more, bodies are, in an ugly but apt word, 'informatized'. In numerous surveillance situations, bodies are reduced to data, perhaps most obviously through the use of biometrics at borders. Yet in this paradigmatic case, the end in view is to verify the identity of the body, indeed, of the person, to permit them to cross the border (or not). One cannot but conclude that information *about* that body is being treated as if it were conclusive in determining the *identity* of the person. If the distinction is maintained, then one might worry about whether or not the fingerprint or iris scan adequately enrols the person in the system, while ignoring what Irma van der Ploeg calls 'bodily integrity'.[96] In condensed form, this is the story of how disembodied information ends up critically affecting the life chances of flesh-and-blood migrants, asylum-seekers and the like.[97]

Now, I think that this gives another, surveillance-oriented twist to what you say about adiaphorization, those actions made exempt from ethical evaluation through technical means. Electronic mediation enables a further distancing between the actor and the outcome than could ever have been imagined in pre-digital bureaucracy. But it also rests on a shrivelled-up and scarcely recognizable notion of 'information' that has been pried free from the person. Because I think that adiaphorization is of the essence here, this seems like a good place to start. Before we're done, however, I would also like us to approach these issues from the other end, as it were; from the perspective of an ethics of care. May we begin by probing surveillance adiaphorically?

Zygmunt Bauman Hitting the bull's eye again, David; your intuition as to other surveillance–morality interfaces beyond those signalled by Gary Marx, including an interface yet more seminal and calling for yet more inquisitive attention, is as correct as it is timely. To start with, it would never have occurred to Bentham that tempting and seducing were the keys to the panopticon's efficiency in eliciting desirable behaviour. There was no carrot, just a stick, in the panopticon's toolbox. Panopticon-style surveillance assumes that the road to submission to an offer leads through the elimination of choice. Our market-deployed surveillance assumes that manipulation of choice (through seduction, not coercion) is the surest way to clear the offers through demand. The willing, nay enthusiastic, cooperation of the manipulated is the paramount resource deployed by the synopticons of consumer markets.

This was, though, a side-remark, but perhaps apposite if we wish to set the scene for your major inquiry. Decomposing, slicing, pulverizing totalities into an aggregate of traits that can then be recomposed back (but also, in principle, rearranged and composed into a different 'totality') is not an invention of police or border control. Neither is it an idiosyncrasy of totalitarian powers or more generally power-obsessed regimes. Particularly if viewed in retrospect, it seems to be a general attribute of the modern way of life (known for its obsession with differentiation, classification and files), now massively redeployed for a radically changed strategy in the course of the transition to the liquid modern society of consumers: redeployed for the sake of including 'free choice' in the marketing strategy, or more precisely, rendering servitude voluntary and making submission be lived through as an advance in freedom and testimony to the chooser's autonomy (I have described that process elsewhere, dubbing it 'subjectivity fetishism').[98]

A somewhat extreme and perhaps too off-puttingly blatant, but fairly characteristic example is provided by the universal habit of dating agencies of arranging the potential objects of desire according to the preferences stated by potential clients – like colour of skin or hair, height, breast size, declared interests, favourite pastimes etc. The tacit assumption is that human beings seeking the agency's assistance in their search for human companions need to and can compose them out of their selection of traits. In the course of that 'decomposition for the sake of recomposition', something vital disappears from view and from mind and to all practical intents and purposes is lost: namely, the 'human person', 'the Other' of morality, the subject in his or her own right and the object of my responsibility. You are right to be worried here, David. When another human is treated along the lines of a commodity good selected according to colour, size and number of add-ups, adiaphorization is in full swing and at its most devastating. An assembly of traits, whether animate or inanimate, can hardly be a moral object, whose treatment is subjected to moral judgement. That applies to dating agencies in the same measure as to policing agencies, even if widely different purposes are ostensibly pursued. Whatever the manifest function of the exercise, the latent yet undetachable function is exclusion of the object of decomposition/recomposition from the class of morally relevant entities and the universe of moral obligations. In other words, the adiaphorization of their treatment.

DL Yes, once again, I fear you're right. Ironically though, surveillance – someone to watch over me – may well be valued and sought after in the vicissitudes of liquid modern life. Unfortunately (to put it mildly), however, that 'someone' is all too often some*thing*. And the something is supposedly disembodied information, sorting by means of software and statistical technique. It's the product of double adiaphorization, such that not only is responsibility removed from the process of categorizing, but the very concept of information itself reduces the humanity of the categorized, whether the end in view is dating or killing.

In other words, those collaborative filters and even, ironically, those relational databases tend in some circumstances to deny or at least obscure our human relationality. If, as Levinas teaches us, our humanity is discovered only in the face of the Other, indeed in recognizing our responsibility to the Other, then there's something deeply disturbing about surveillance systems that seem to tear such relationality apart or even, more subtly, to erode it bit by bit. But should we not have expected just this, if, as many agree, one of the turning points towards modern surveillance was the dire architectural diagram known as the panopticon?

Jeremy Bentham was among other things a secular prison reformer in an age when prominent opinion about what was wrong with places of punishment included many Christian voices (not to mention others who advocated shipping offenders to penal colonies on the far side of the world). I've often wondered whether Bentham was not only aware of this but also tried to head off criticism of his plan by quoting as an epigraph the biblical Psalm 139 which is all about God's all-seeing eye. But Bentham's reading of God's eye stresses only the apparently controlling, instrumental gaze of an invisible, inscrutable and possibly punitive deity. Bentham saw only the blinkered rational vision of Enlightenment.

A fairer reading of the psalm reveals another kind of seeing altogether, a relational vision that supports and protects; 'even there your hand will guide me, your right hand will hold me fast' (Psalm 139: 10). For sure, there is moral direction here but the contextual analogy is the warmly watchful eye of the friend, the parent. I find in this other reading of Bentham's epigraphical psalm

138

the embryo of a critical ethics of care. Not necessarily or primarily to seek alternative surveillance practices so much as to probe existing practices with a view to exposing their actual effects. This is the kind of exercise engaged in by Lucas Introna when he shows how the distancing effect of the screen can 'de-face' the Other by 'screening out' all but its categories.[99] I find real promise in such 'disclosive' ethics.

ZB I am not sure that Bentham's vision of Enlightenment was, as you say, blinkered. It was, after all, perfectly in tune with the most central, indeed defining precepts of the Enlightenment: putting world affairs under human management and replacing providence ('blind' fate, 'random' contingency) with Reason, that mortal enemy of accidents, ambiguity, ambivalence and inconsistency. I am tempted to say that Bentham's panopticon was a bricks-and-mortar version of the Enlightenment's spirit.

A less advertised, though no less paramount aspect of those twin Enlightenment precepts was the assumption of the moral ignorance and incapacity of the hoi polloi, the 'ordinary folk' (variously branded 'the people' or 'the masses'): as Rousseau (somewhat too bluntly) proclaimed, people must be forced to be free . . . A moral crusade needs to rely on people's obedience or their greed, not on their doubtful moral impulses. It is for that reason, I believe, that voluntary enlistment in the war declared against the vagaries of fate was not widely expected; the wager was on codifying the duties, rather than unleashing the liberties of choice. This is why Bentham, and the pioneers of the 'satanic mills', and Frederick Taylor of the time-and-motion measurements that aimed to reduce the machine operator to the role of its obedient slave, could sincerely believe themselves to be the agents, promoters and executive arms of morality – in the sense of both interpretations of Psalm 139: 10: watching, and guiding in the right direction . . . Together with all other enterprises and gambits, the matter of grounding morality was the task, and prerogative, of managers. It was managerial reason, of the managers caught in motion and recorded in James Burnham's *The Managerial Revolution* (1939), that spoke through Jeremy Bentham's, and still Henry Ford's, lips.

Today, however, we've left behind the dictatorial and ethical ambitions of Burnham-style managers. We've left them behind as a result of the 'managerial revolution mark two' – the managers having discovered a much better (less costly as well as less burdensome and unwieldy, and potentially more profitable) recipe for control and domination: hiring out managerial duties to the managed themselves, transferring the task of keeping them in line from debit to credit, from liabilities to assets, from costs to gains – by 'subsidiarizing' that task to those at the receiving end of the operation. This is something that IKEA is famous for – leaving the assembly of factory-produced elements to clients paying for the privilege of doing the job, instead of being remunerated for its performance – but it is a principle ever more widely deployed in shaping the present-day patterns of the domination/subordination relationship.

The avenue for a re-ethicalizing of those patterns signalled in your last paragraph with reference to Lucas Introna is as emboldening and hopeful as anything still to be tested in practice – but let's never forget, taught as we are by a long string of false dawns and bitter awakenings in the past, that the lines separating 'care' from 'dependence', and 'freedom' from 'abandonment', are endemically contentious; each apparent opposition seems more like a couple of inseparable (indeed, complementary) aspects of the same relationship. To put it simply: yes, surveillance may quash some moral scruples by manifesting its 'care applications'. But at a price – not at all morally innocent. And without stopping being surveillance and without putting paid to the moral doubts with which it has been, not unjustly, associated. We are still waiting in vain for a cake we can eat and have . . . even if its discovery is announced again with each successive technological novelty.

7

Agency and hope

David Lyon Having read through our conversation thus far I would like us to confront a couple of issues that have appeared several times but which we have stopped short of discussing at any length. If I may, I'd like to signal these with the words 'agency' and 'hope'. The first is very salient to surveillance and connects with your remark to Peter Beilharz in 2001,[100] that Gramsci showed you how women and men are far from unconscious of how society works and should never be considered mere victims of social structures, however strong those appear. Some surveillance studies seem to suggest that human beings are just bound by the bureaucratic web, caught in the camera lens, or helplessly tracked and trailed by their own cellphones. So where can agency be found, or fostered?

The second may be connected with the first, especially in so far as, still following Gramsci, your work indicates how things could be different. Human beings can and do make a difference, think outside the box and sometimes even change the course of history in the direction of justice and solidarity. For all that might be said about the ways that power evaporates into the space of flows, or how homeland security prompts profoundly racist policies and practices and succeeds in casting the net so widely that we're all 'categorical' suspects, or even the growing complacency about the general loss of control over our personal information, I don't believe that all is lost. But what are the grounds for such hope? How is it tempered by uncertainty, ambivalence or even suspicion? And how can it contribute to what you call those vital choices between lives human and inhuman?

Zygmunt Bauman 'All is lost' only when (if!) we believe this to be true (W. I. Thomas close to a hundred years ago found out that much, concluding that 'once people believe that something is true it tends to become true in consequence of their actions'). But even then not all is lost – the non-acceptance of such a situation, even if it is chased down to the dungeons of the subconscious and incarcerated there, burrows a wide opening in that conviction through which miracles are invited to flow and indeed do . . . I suppose that it is intrinsically impossible to live with the belief that 'all is lost'; and that it is also inconceivable, assuming that humans constitute an endemically transgressive species and cannot be otherwise, having been blessed or cursed with a language containing the particle 'no' (that is, the possibility of denying or refuting what is) and the future tense (that is, the ability to be moved by a vision of a reality that doesn't exist 'as yet' but might in 'a future' with the same force as other animals are moved by the evidence supplied by their senses). In a choosing, transcending, transgressing animal like homo sapiens no condition is fully and truly of an 'all is lost' kind. Which does not mean, though, that making words flesh is a straightforward operation, assured of success, or that a foolproof (and above all uncontentious) recipe for the exit from trouble lies waiting to be found, or that once it is found it would be seen through in concert and to universal applause. But let me send you again to what we've briefly discussed with reference to a recent Houellebecq interview . . .

Another point: the nation-state is not the only 'agency in crisis'. Another 'agency in crisis' is the individual, called, encouraged and expected to find (as Ulrich Beck repeatedly reminds us) 'individual solutions to socially generated problems'. We are all now 'individuals' courtesy of that decree – unwritten, yet deeply engraved into all or nearly all social practices. We are all 'individuals de jure' – yet most of us on many an occasion find ourselves far short of the status of an 'individual de facto' (because of a deficit of knowledge and skills or resources, or simply because the 'problems' we confront could only be 'resolved' collectively, not single-handedly: by concerted and coordinated action by the many). But we are unlikely to be forgiven for that gap between social expectations (also internalized by us) and our practical abilities – neither by so-called 'public opinion' nor by our own (even though socially groomed) conscience. I guess that this deeply humiliating sense, denying self-dignity and hope of redemption, of having been cast in a state of inescapable and unredeemable disqualification is the most powerful stimulus to the present-day version of 'voluntary servitude' (our cooperation with electronic/ digital surveillance); a version that in the last account is nothing more, though also nothing less, than a desperate attempt to escape abandonment to loneliness, read impotence. We may be 'bound' and 'caught', but we also 'jump in', plunge and dive in of our own will, in our hope's last stand.

DL   If so, then hope's last stand may not last long! How could it? And where, in liquid times, can one really 'stand'? I'm with you on the tectonic shifts that render modernity far less solid than it once appeared – even though Marx and others did warn us long ago that the apparent solidity 'melts into air' – with on the one hand the ambivalence evident all around, and on the other the merely 'manufactured certainties' of risk societies. No wonder hope hides its face and even its feeble fill-in, optimism, waits in the wings for some semblance of a cultural cue that will allow it a moment on the unwelcoming stage of liquid times.

The flows of digital information and images that we're discussing in the context of surveillance are everywhere magnifying that sense of liquidity, which also, according to some, has the effect of 'cooling' memories. The 'hot' memories that might shape and direct cultural development in properly ethical ways are replaced by the coolness of paying attention to the incoming email, the status update and the revised forecast, as they flit across our consciousness.[101] Even in the realm of surveillance, as your 'plunge and dive' metaphor reminds us, things are in constant flux. There, too, consumer statuses alter with each new bit of transactional information and your chances of being detained for further questioning at the airport vary with traffic levels and the most recent trail of traces you've left in your wake.

That's why, in a world where the social sciences so often have – appropriate! – recourse to a hermeneutic of suspicion, I turn to your writings, redolent with reminders that hermeneutics can also be sought in retrieval. While we may steel ourselves to live with ambivalence or recoil from dreams of the digital sublime, are there not also opportunities to consider what may be recovered from culturally neglected vocabularies, without slipping into nostalgia or reaction? I remember with gratitude, for example, attending a seminar in 1996 with Jacques Derrida as he let the light shine from Levinas's exposition of *la responsabilité*.[102] That helped revive my own halting hope that there are alternatives that also make sense of the present liquid times.

This is a hermeneutic of retrieval, as I see it, because it reaches back in order to confront and engage the present, while at the same time holding to a hope of what (as you reminded us with Paul's words) we cannot yet see. In the world of surveillant vision, if the panoptic gaze objectifies the Other then Levinas prompts us to see that this does not shut out the possibilities for another kind of gaze. Vision does not necessarily 'blind us to the humanity of the other'.[103] Levinas leads us back to the Other of the Torah, as the alien or stranger, the widow and the orphan. And who in biblical history stands more starkly for the marginalized outsider than Hagar, the estranged wife cruelly cast out by Abraham and Sarah? Her subordinate gender and inferior ethnicity do not go unnoticed by *YHWH* whom she acknowledges gratefully as 'the God who *sees* me'. The loving gaze and liberating action are inseparable in this account.[104] Another way is possible, pregnant with hope.

ZB Why did I resort to such a dramatic sobriquet as 'hope's last stand'? Because of the crisis of agency, the present predicament's most conspicuous bane. Hope nowadays feels frail, vulnerable, fissiparous precisely because we can't locate a viable and sufficiently potent agency that can be relied on to make the words flesh. This difficulty, as I go on repeating, is in its turn due to the looming divorce of the power to have things done and the power able to secure that the right things are done and the wrong things undone (we used to call that second power 'politics'). The extant political agencies (fixed by the state government) are all well short of matching the grandiosity of the tasks. Our political leaders agree on Friday what is to be done, and then spend the weekend trembling until the opening of the stock exchanges on Monday, to learn what in fact they have (more correctly, what has in fact been) done . . . No wonder that suggestions that alternative agencies are being born that are itching to join in the fray are so avidly consumed – and therefore so plentiful. Perhaps the internet will do what the change of the party in government failed to achieve? Perhaps better surveillance gadgets will accomplish what years of moral preaching and composing ethical codes did not? We *hope for hope* – for a better grounded, more hopeful hope . . . In the digital facility to summon thousands of men and women to a public square we try hard to spy out a promise of constructing a new regime that will put paid to the oddities and inanities of the present one. This is OK, and for our mental sanity most welcome, as long as we go on hoping; it is much less helpful when we proclaim (or accept others' proclamations) that the case that such a regime will fulfil it successfully has already been opened and closed.

You are fully right as to Levinas's vision, but what would Levinas say of the chances of his vision gaining ground in reality if it had to ride the vehicles of electronic and digital surveillance? Both the axe and the razor are exquisite products of technology – but woe to those using them without discretion. Can one shave with an axe? Can one hew wood with a razor? (Though one can use both axe and razor, not exactly in agreement with their original purposes, for killing.) After all, electronic surveillance, as no one has shown more convincingly than David Lyon, splits and 'demographizes' what Levinas's 'Face of the Other' synthesizes and makes whole . . .

Gérard Berry, one of the leading French experts on the social effects of informatics, told his interviewer Roger-Pol Droit the story of when he met Tunisian teenagers just after the latest revolution.[105] He told them how difficult it was when he was their age to call together even a small gathering. His conversationalists were astonished and amused. They had never visualized such a world, and never tried to think in its terms. On the other hand, Berry was similarly astonished and amused when he tried to extract from those teenagers a story of how they 'came' to use electronic means of composing and decomposing their 'togethernesses'. He did not get an answer – and realized that the question was the wrong one to address to those youngsters. They had never lived in a world that did not contain Facebook and Twitter – and so they never 'came' to using Facebook and its ilk to construct and deconstruct their social world.

The only social world they knew and had learned to inhabit was digitally operated. For them, the internet was as natural as the sea or a mountain, so Berry concluded, and they knew nothing to compare it with to evaluate its relative merits or vices. Pressed by Droit to predict where we go from here, Berry was seemingly ill at ease. Your GPS (global positioning system), he suggested, will

> perpetually transmit your coordinates, and your computer your clicks, which will permit measurement of the variations of collective and individual behaviour, but also of quantities of information which could become wholly dangerous for democracy. If people are not made aware now, these dangerous practices will be in place before the right questions can be asked, and the normal democratic debate will not take place, it will be too late.

Well, shall we agree, at least for the time being (until a time when firmer and less ambiguous evidence has been made available by the people's history-making), that digital surveillance is a sharp sword which we don't as yet know how to blunt – and obviously a double-edged sword which we don't as yet know how to handle safely?

As to our hopes: hope is one human quality we are bound never to lose without losing our humanity. But we may be similarly certain that a safe haven in which to drop its anchor will take a very long time to be found. You, like the rest of us, know all about the fate of the little shepherd who cried wolf once too often . . . But what we tend to know less about, while forgetting it more easily, is that a similar fate awaits any one of us who cries once too often, from the height of a crow's nest, 'the promised land ahead!'

DL As with our earlier conversations, this one will remain properly open-ended. But your ringing comments provoke me to press for more, one last time. Yes, hope and humanness are inseparable, and yes, finding a safe anchorage may take time (and, one might add, appears even more elusive in liquid times). But if the boy who cried wolf warned of non-existent dangers, then what of those who might announce the 'promised land'? The wolf story stresses the importance of truth-telling so that all should only be alerted to real risks. We've touched on several opposite instances, where foolish futuristic claims are made about the transformative promise of technology (for example). And without hesitation we can agree that such vacuous optimism is as false as the feared wolf in the ancient story. But isn't more possible?

May I share with you an instance where I have found real direction – which I am persuaded derives from hope – in my own attempts to understand surveillance? These convictions are not common currency in the overt writing of sociology or history, but they, or their equivalents, are nonetheless present, quietly in the background. They cannot be proved (whatever that means) but they cannot but be presupposed. We all rely, like it or not, on such 'metatheoretical' assumptions.

When I was first grappling with post-9/11 surveillance, I was trying to get to grips with the ballooning exclusionary emphases of security-surveillance initiatives. A newly clear vocabulary was taking shape in the media and politics that singled out 'Muslim', 'Arab', 'Middle Eastern' as proscribed categories. As Bourdieu simply but sagely says, 'the fate of groups is bound up with the words that designate them',[106] and now we know just how profoundly consequential it is for those designations to be associated with the word 'terrorist'. This is exclusion through domination, where the excluded are placed outside normal (and in this case legal) life. But as theologian Miroslav Volf observes,[107] other exclusions include elimination (think Bosnia, Rwanda) and its softer sister, assimilation (you can survive among us if you renounce your identity – this week the Canadian government announced that women may not wear the *niqab* at a citizenship ceremony). Then there's exclusion by abandonment, which we've discussed in relation to flawed consumers, for example. We now know how to automate 'walking by on the other side'.

Poignantly, Volf came to explore these matters when he was challenged by Jürgen Moltmann as to whether he, a Croatian, could ever embrace a četnik – the name for Serbian fighters who had desolated his native country. As a Christian, he unambiguously hopes for the time when swords will be beaten into ploughshares but recognizes that for the present the question is '*how to live under the rule of Caesar in the absence of the reign of truth and justice?*' (his emphasis).[108] He quotes Hans Enzenberger (in order to go beyond him) to the effect that Sisyphus' stone, which he was condemned to keep pushing up the hill, is called 'peace'. Small, neighbourly acts must be carried out even though the killer might return at any moment. But, says Volf, those who 'carry the cross' in the Messiah's footsteps 'are to break the cycle of violence by refusing to be caught in the automatism of revenge' such that 'the costly acts of nonretaliation become a seed from which the fragile fruit of Pentecostal peace grows . . . '[109]

Now my point in mentioning this is that such deep convictions inform social analysis and historiography. Even though we may disagree with the beliefs in which they originate, can we not still form strategic alliances with others that affirm, for instance, agency and hope? Kieran Flanagan has noted, and I concur, that your work, Zygmunt, 'gives an unexpected witness to . . . theological resonances in modernity'.[110] I think he means 'unexpected' in the sense that you are highly dubious about God's activity in the world and deeply critical (as I am) of many manifestations of 'religious' sentiment. But he's right that you boldly acknowledge the significance of themes all too often left only to theologians – the reality of evil, the inescapability of ethics, the robustness of long-term relationships, the self-giving Other and the priority of neighbour-love, the conundrums of mortality . . . several of which we've touched on here.

I find myself walking unapologetically and without regret in the Christian tradition, while referring to your work just because it articulates ideas, nay commitments, that lie very close to my own. Your work comports so well with things I hold dear that I have found I can continue to travel far in your company, even though we may also find moments of tension or, ultimately, basic difference. I discover that sometimes you quote approvingly Christian sources and they – including Volf – acknowledge their debt to your wisdom. As Levinas would say, there's some *rashimo*, that idea of the Kabbalah, in your work that echoes the shrewdness and lucidity of the Holy Books, sparking and spurring the conscience and driving us in new directions.

So, liquid surveillance? Well, yes, because it's crucial that we grasp the new ways that surveillance is seeping into the bloodstream of contemporary life *and* that the ways it does so correspond to the currents of liquid modernity. But the idea of liquidity comes from the pen of one who resolutely refuses the shallowness and superficiality of much social theory and turns instead to the themes to which I've just made reference. I guess my question is, how far can social and political theory remain open to the contributions of those who speak from within religious traditions? Who, for instance, find in ancient Judaism and Christianity the roots of the idea that the test of good governance is how the most vulnerable or those with the weakest voices are treated. Or who dare to hope, not for some utopia of merely human manufacture, but for the fulfilment of the words of the sages, the promises of past prophets, or even, to repeat words often used by you, the 'word made flesh'.

ZB As so many times before in our conversation, you've unerringly put your finger on the most vulnerable, jarring and festering spots and aspects of the issue. In my little study of the 'art of life' I suggested that it is fate (the generic name for everything we can't prevent or even significantly alter) that sets the range of our available and realistic options, but that it is our character (the generic name for what we can try to consciously control, change or cultivate) that selects among the options. The co-presence and interplay of these two largely autonomous factors render human deeds underdetermined and, in the end, never fully predictable: even the Nazis and the Communists, in their concentration camps, did not succeed in fully eliminating human choices! You and I as everyone else around, from the most distant past and on to eternity, was, is and will remain *homo eligens* – a choosing being, making history as she or he is made by it . . .

And because I am convinced of all that, I believe

simultaneously in the possibility and inevitability of morality. We will never forget what Eve and Adam learnt when they tasted the fruit of the Tree of Knowledge of Good and Evil . . . It is just that each set of circumstances combining into 'fate' attaches different sanctions to different choices. Which means that under differing circumstances the probabilities of certain choices differ: while, being *homini sapienti* in addition to *homini eligenti*, we are likely to give preference to the less costly choices over the more expensive ones (whatever the currency in which the relative costs and gains are measured). But there is a huge distance between determination and probability, and it is in that poorly marked space that character operates – in company with morality. I keep repeating that 'to be moral' is many things, but it is most certainly not a recipe for an easy and comfortable life. Uncertainty (and an uncertainty of the most harrowing kind: an irremovable and irreducible uncertainty *before* a choice is considered and *after* it has been made) is the home ground, the natural habitat of morality. And all too often, morality (contrary to the teachings of almost all modern ethical philosophers) lies not in *conforming* to binding and well-nigh universally accepted and obeyed norms, but in staunch *resistance* to them – at enormous personal cost to the resistor . . .

I guess there is an 'elective affinity' between the above belief and the credo of the late Tony Judt. The day after his death, I noted the following thoughts in my diary: 'If we have learned nothing else from the twentieth century', Judt insisted, 'we should at least have grasped that the more perfect the answer, the more terrifying the consequences. Incremental improvements upon unsatisfactory circumstances are the best that we can hope for, and probably all we should seek.' History, in other words, can teach us humility and recommend modesty in our undertakings. On the other hand, it won't dash our hopes – so long as we listen to its advice. In a conversation with David Foley of the *Independent* Judt presented his creed:

> I was asked the other day if I see a slide into something like authoritarianism or totalitarianism. I don't see that. In a way I see something much more corrosive, which is a loss of conviction, a loss of faith in the culture of open democracy, a sense of scepticism and withdrawal which is probably quite far advanced on both sides of the Atlantic . . . But I also think we are likely to see within the next half-generation a resurgence of political enthusiasm in the form of protests of political anger, of organization among young people, at the stagnation of the last 25 years. So medium term optimism, short term pessimism.[111]

To endorse and retrospectively justify Judt's 'medium term optimism', the future – not immediately but relatively soon – will have to navigate between the Scylla of resurrecting the past and the Charybdis of a light-hearted dismissal of its legacy. 'It would be pleasing – but misleading – to report that social democracy, or something like it, represents the future that we would paint for ourselves in an ideal world,' declared Judt on a separate occasion, 'carefully pronouncing every word', as his interviewer Evan R. Goldstein comments.[112] To abandon the gains made by social democrats – the New Deal, the Great Society, the European welfare state – 'is to betray those who came before us as well as generations yet to come'.

Currently, though, we are watching the decline of eighty years of great investment in public services. We are throwing away the efforts, ideas and ambitions of the past. In throwing out the bad answer, we have forgotten the good questions. I want to put the good questions back on the table.

Personally, I suspect that Judt found the meaning he so ardently sought in life, at least in the life of the individual carrying Tony Judt's name, and – in so far as other individual human beings have decided to saturate their lives with a similar meaning – perhaps in human history as well. Judt confessed to Foley:

> The only seriously philosophical conversations I've had have been with the philosopher Thomas Nagel here at [New York University], who's a friend of mine. We've had long conversations about the responsibilities of the living for what happens after they die. In other words not about life after death but about life after one's own death and about the responsibilities one has to the world one leaves behind, in terms of behaviour now, in terms of what one says or tries to achieve and so on . . .
>
> These responsibilities are very substantial. We do die – we don't live after we die, or at least if we do, I don't know anything about it and I have no proof and no arguments to offer in support of it – but we live on in other people in ways for which we are responsible. The memory we leave behind, the impression we leave of the shape of ideas we had, and the reasons people might have for continuing to engage those ideas, are responsibilities that we have now for a world that we can't be responsible for. There are grounds for acting now as though we would live on, as though we were going to be there to take responsibility for our words and our deeds, a sense of living for the future even though it's not your own future.

DL Yes, yes, and this is indeed a further way to conceive of and act on *la responsabilité*. For me, as a believer, I'd only add that the New Testament enjoins us to live in the present now *as if* the future *shalom* had already arrived. We live out now the life of worship, of finding ourselves in the face of the Other, of beating swords to ploughshares, of pressing to enable the voices of the marginalized – the categorically suspect – to be heard, without fearing the consequences of so doing.

ZB 'To live in the present now as if the future *shalom* had already arrived,' you insist . . . This, like other calls from both the Old and the New Testament, was addressed to the saints, including the precept of the unconditionality of responsibility articulated by Levinas, also a believer (but please consider that it would be an awful world if attention to the Testaments' messages and the grace of absorbing them depended on a belief in the divinity of their senders). And the saints received the message, digested it and recycled it into deeds. That is why we call them saints. That is why they are saints. Alas, we can't all be saints. Yet we wouldn't be human without the saints' presence . . . They show us the way (they are the way), they prove to us the path can be taken, they are pangs of conscience for us, we who refuse or are unable to take the path and follow it.

In his latest novel, *The Map and the Territory* (ponder, please, the message in that title!), Michel Houellebecq tries to answer the question of whether William Morris (famous for the precept that 'design and execution should never be separated') was a utopian. He meditates, stoutly refuses to pretend conclusiveness ('I am too old,' he explains, 'I no longer have the desire for or the habit of coming to conclusions'), yet suggests nonetheless: 'What can be said is that the model of society proposed by William Morris certainly would not be utopian in a world where all men were like William Morris.'

I endorse this hypothesis, including all its explicit encouragement and implicit warnings.

Notes

Introduction

1 Gilles Deleuze, 'Postscript on the societies of control', *October* 59 (Winter 1992): 3–7.

2 Kevin Haggerty and Richard Ericson, 'The surveillant assemblage', *British Journal of Sociology* 54: 1 (2000): 605–22.

3 William G. Staples, *Everyday Surveillance: Vigilance and Visibility in Postmodern Life* (Lanham: Rowman & Littlefield, 2008), p. 8 (emphasis added).

4 Zygmunt Bauman, *Liquid Modernity* (Cambridge: Polity, 2000), p. 11.

5 For discussion, see David Lyon, ed., *Theorizing Surveillance: The Panopticon and Beyond* (Cullompton: Willan, 2006).

6 Didier Bigo, 'Security: a field left fallow', in M. Dillon and A. W. Neal, eds, *Foucault on Politics, Security and War* (London: Palgrave Macmillan, 2011), p. 109 (emphasis added). See also David Lyon, 'Everyday surveillance: personal data and

social classification', *Information, Communication, and Society* 5: 1 (2002): 1–16.

7 See, e.g., David Lyon, 'The border is everywhere: ID cards, surveillance and the other', in E. Zureik and M. B. Salter, eds, *Global Surveillance and Policing* (Cullompton: Willan, 2005), pp. 66–82.

8 Bauman discusses adiaphorization in several writings, including *Postmodern Ethics* (Oxford: Blackwell, 1993).

9 See, e.g., Oscar Gandy, *Coming to Terms with Chance: Engaging Rational Discrimination and Cumulative Disadvantage* (Farnham: Ashgate, 2009).

10 David Lyon, *Surveillance Studies: An Overview* (Cambridge: Polity, 2007), p. 32.

11 Daniel Solove, *The Digital Person: Technology and Privacy in the Information Age* (New York: New York University Press, 2004), p. 47.

12 Bauman, *Liquid Modernity*, p. 10.

13 Ibid., p. 11.

14 See, e.g., Katja Franko Aas, *Sentencing in the Age of Information* (London: Glass House, 2005), ch. 4.

15 David Lyon, ed., *Surveillance as Social Sorting: Privacy, Risk, and Digital Discrimination* (London: Routledge, 2003).

16 See, e.g., Anna Vemer Andrzejewski, *Building Power: Architecture and Surveillance in Victorian America* (Knoxville: University of Tennessee Press, 2008).

17 Gandy, *Coming to Terms with Chance*.

18 See, e.g., *Work, Consumerism and the New Poor* (Buckingham: Open University Press, 1998).

Chapter 1

19 Elisabeth Bumiller and Thom Shanker, 'War evolves with drones, some tiny as bugs', *New York Times*, 19 June 2011.

20 Brian Stelter, 'Now drones are absolute', at http://motherboard.vice.com.

21 This particular claim of theft, like most of those made and contested during the California 'gold rush' of 1849 and thereafter, did not find unambiguous resolution in the courts; but then the internet at the start of the twenty-first century, like California in the middle of the nineteenth, was a uniquely lawless place – without private property, licensing fees or taxes.

22 Josh Rose, 'How social media is having a positive impact on our culture', 23 Feb. 2011, at http://mashable.com/2011/02/23/social-media-culture/ (accessed Mar. 2012).

23 Georg Simmel, 'The sociology of secrecy and of the secret societies', *American Journal of Sociology* 11 (1906): 441–98.

24 Gary T. Marx with Glenn W. Muschert, 'Simmel on secrecy: a legacy and inheritance for the sociology of information', in Christian Papiloud and Cécile Rol, eds, *The Possibility of Sociology* (Wiesbaden: VS Verlag für Sozialwissenschaften, 2008).

25 See Paul Lewis, 'Teenage networking websites face anti-paedophile investigation', *Guardian*, 3 July 2006.

26 Eugène Enriquez, 'L'idéal type de l'individu hypermoderne: l'individu pervers?', in Nicole Aubert, ed., *L'Individu hypermoderne* (Toulouse: Érès, 2004), p. 49.

27 Siegfried Kracauer, *Die Angestellen*, essays first serialized in the *Frankfurter Allgemeine Zeitung* through 1929, and published in a book form by Suhrkamp in 1930. Here quoted in Quintin Hoare's translation: Siegfried Kracauer, *The Salaried Masses: Duty and Distraction in Weimar Germany* (London: Verso, 1998), p. 39.

28 Germaine Greer, *The Future of Feminism*, Dr J. Tans Lecture (Maastricht: Studium Generale, Maastricht University, 2004), p. 13.

29 Sherry Turkle, *Alone Together: Why We Expect More of Technology and Less of Each Other* (New York: Basic Books, 2011), p. xii.

30 Daniel Trottier, *Social Media as Surveillance: Rethinking Visibility in a Converging World* (London: Ashgate, 2012).

31 Other scholars have arrived at different limits, sometimes twice as large as Dunbar's. According to a recent entry to Wikipedia, 'anthropologist H. Russell Bernard and Peter Killworth and associates have done a variety of field studies in the United States that came up with an estimated mean number of ties – 290 – that is roughly double Dunbar's estimate. The Bernard-Killworth median of 231 is lower, due to upward straggle in the distribution: this is still appreciably larger than Dunbar's estimate. The Bernard-Killworth estimate of the maximum likelihood of the size of a person's social network is based on a number of field studies using different methods in various populations. It is not an average of study averages but a repeated finding. Nevertheless, the Bernard-Killworth number has not been popularized as widely as Dunbar's.' Unlike the

researchers named above, who focus on groupings in various contemporary human populations, the prime objects of Dunbar's field and archive studies and the suppliers of the raw data from which Dunbar's number was calculated were primates and pleistocene populations; therefore, Dunbar's proposition – that given the structure of the neocortex shared by primates and their younger human relatives, the size of the primeval horde sets the limits to the number of 'meaningful relationships' for humans – needs to be taken as an assumption rather than a corroborated finding.

32 See 'McDonald's #McDStories Twitter campaign backfires', *Daily Telegraph*, 24 June 2012, at www.telegraph.co.uk (accessed Apr. 2012).

33 On this, see the thoughtful article by Malcolm Gladwell, 'Small change: why the revolution will not be tweeted', *New Yorker*, 24 Oct. 2010.

34 See Jean-Claude Kaufmann, *Sex@mour* (Paris: Armand Colin, 2010), here quoted from David Macey's translation, *Love Online* (Cambridge: Polity, 2012).

Chapter 2

35 Kevin Haggerty, 'Tear down the walls', in Lyon, *Theorizing Surveillance*.

36 Michel Foucault, *Discipline and Punish* (New York: Vintage, 1977), pp. 202–3.

37 Oscar Gandy, *The Panoptic Sort: A Political Economy of Personal Information* (Boulder: Westview, 1993).

38 Lorna Rhodes, 'Panoptical intimacies', *Public Culture* 10: 2 (1998): 308.

39 Lorna Rhodes, *Total Confinement: Madness and Reason in the Maximum Security Prison* (Berkeley: University of California Press, 2004).

40 Mark Andrejevic, *Reality TV: The Work of Being Watched* (New York: Rowman & Littlefield, 2004).

41 This is a near quote from David Lyon, 'The search for surveillance theories', in Lyon, *Theorizing Surveillance*, p. 8.

42 Loïc Wacquant, *Punishing the Poor: The Neoliberal Government of Social Insecurity* (Durham: Duke University Press, 2008), p. 25.

43 John Gilliom, *Overseers of the Poor* (Chicago: University of Chicago Press, 2005).

44 Didier Bigo, 'Globalized (in)security: the field and the ban-opticon', in Naoki Sakai and Jon Solomon, eds, *Traces 4: Translation, Biopolitics, Colonial Difference* (Hong Kong: Hong Kong University Press, 2006).

45 Michel Agier, *Le Couloir des exiles. Être étranger dans un monde commun* (Marseille: Éditions du Croquant, 2011).

46 Lyon, *Surveillance Studies*, p. 42.

47 Oscar Gandy, 'Coming to terms with the panoptic sort', in David Lyon and Elia Zureik, eds, *Computers, Surveillance and Privacy* (Minneapolis: University of Minnesota Press, 1996), p. 152.

48 Mark Andrejevic, *iSpy: Surveillance and Power in the Interactive Era* (Lawrence: University of Kansas Press, 2007), p. 125.

49 Gandy, *Coming to Terms with Chance*.

50 Geoff Bowker and Susan Leigh Star, *Sorting Things Out* (Cambridge, MA: MIT Press, 1999).

51 Thomas Mathiesen, 'The viewer society: Michel

Foucault's panopticon revisited', *Theoretical Criminology* 1: 2 (1997): 215–34.

52 See David Lyon, '9/11, synopticon, and scopophilia: watching and being watched', in Kevin D. Haggerty and Richard V. Ericson, eds, *The New Politics of Surveillance and Visibility* (Toronto: University of Toronto Press, 2006), pp. 35–54.

53 Aaron Doyle, 'Revisiting the synopticon: reconsidering Mathiesen's "viewer society" in the age of web 2.0', *Theoretical Criminology* 15: 3 (2011): 283–99.

54 Zygmunt Bauman, *Collateral Damage: Social Inequalities in a Global Age* (Cambridge: Polity, 2011), pp. 46–7.

Chapter 3

55 Götz Aly and Susanne Heim, *Vordenker der Vernichtung. Auschwitz und die deutschen Pläne für die neue europäische Ordnung* (Hamburg: Hoffmann & Campe, 1991), pp. 14, 482. 'What was initially a small office established on 6th October 1939 with the brief to coordinate "resettlement of European nations" [Reichskommisariat für die Festigung Deutschen Volkstums] swiftly turned into a powerful institution with numerous branches, employing in addition to its officers thousands of ethnographers, architects, agronomists, accountants and specialists of all imaginable scientific disciplines' (pp. 125–6). (The book was translated as Götz Aly and Susanne Heim, *Architects of Annihilation: Auschwitz and the Logic of Destruction* (London: Weidenfeld & Nicolson, 2001.) See also Götz Aly's reply to Dan Diner, *Vierteljahreshefte für Zeitgeschichte* 4 (1993).

56 Cf. Klaus Dörner, *Tödliches Mitleid. Zur Frage der Unerträglichkeit des Lebens* (Gütersloh: Paranus, 1988), pp. 13, 65.

57 Thom Shanker and Matt Richtel, 'In new military, data overload can be deadly', *New York Times*, 16 Jan. 2011.

58 See Günther Anders, *Le temps de la fin* (1960; Paris: L'Herne, 2007), pp. 52–3.

59 Lyon, 'The border is everywhere'.

60 Ibid.

61 See, e.g., Elisabeth Bumiller, 'Air force drone operators report high levels of stress', *New York Times*, 18 Dec. 2011. At http://www.nytimes.com/2011/12/19/world/asia/air-force-drone-operators-show-high-levels-of-stress.html?_r=3 (accessed Mar. 2012).

62 Roger Silverstone, 'Proper distance: towards an ethics for cyberspace', in Gunnar Liestøl et al., eds, *Digital Media Revisited: Theoretical and Conceptual Innovations in Digital Domains* (Cambridge, MA: MIT Press, 2003), pp. 469–90.

Chapter 4

63 Zygmunt Bauman, *Liquid Fear* (Cambridge: Polity, 2006), p. 6.

64 Ibid., p. 123.

65 Katja Franko Aas, Helene Oppen Gundhus and Heidi Mork Lomell, eds, *Technologies of InSecurity: The Surveillance of Everyday Life* (London: Routledge, 2007), p. 1.

66 Torin Monahan, *Surveillance in the Time of Insecurity* (New Brunswick: Rutgers University Press, 2010), p. 150.

67 Anna Minton, *Ground Control: Fear and Happiness*

in the Twenty-First Century City (London: Penguin, 2011), p. 171.

68 Bigo, 'Security'.

69 Zygmunt Bauman, 'Conclusion: the triple challenge', in Mark Davis and Keith Tester, eds, *Bauman's Challenge: Sociological Issues for the Twenty-First Century* (London: Palgrave Macmillan, 2010), p. 204.

70 'Michel Houellebecq, the art of fiction no. 206', *Paris Review*, no. 194 (Fall 2000). At www.theparisreview.org/interviews/6040/the-art-of-fiction-no-206-michel-houellebecq (accessed Apr. 2012).

71 Solove, *The Digital Person*, p. 47.

72 Vincent Mosco, *The Digital Sublime: Myth, Power and Cyberspace* (Cambridge, MA: MIT Press, 2004).

73 S. F. Murray, 'Battle command: decision-making and the battlefield panopticon', *Military Review* (July–Aug. 2006): 46–51; cited in Kevin Haggerty, 'Visible war: surveillance, speed and information war', in Haggerty and Ericson, *The New Politics*.

74 Zygmunt Bauman, *Socialism: The Active Utopia* (London: Allen & Unwin, 1976), p. 141.

75 Keith Tester, *The Social Thought of Zygmunt Bauman* (London: Palgrave Macmillan, 2004), p. 147.

76 Keith Tester, *Conversations with Zygmunt Bauman* (Cambridge: Polity, 2000), p. 9.

77 David Noble, *The Religion of Technology: The Divinity of Man and the Spirit of Invention* (New York: Penguin, 1997).

78 I tried to express this in, e.g., David Lyon,

Surveillance after September 11 (Cambridge: Polity, 2003), ch. 6.

79 Ibid., p. 166.

Chapter 5

80 Christian Fuchs, Kees Boersma, Anders Albrechtslund and Marisol Sandoval, eds, *Internet and Surveillance* (London: Routledge, 2011), p. xix.

81 Lyon, *Surveillance Studies*, p. 185.

82 See Sachil Singh and David Lyon, 'Surveilling consumers: the social consequences of data processing on Amazon.com', in Russell W. Belk and Rosa Llamas, eds, *The Routledge Companion to Digital Consumption* (London: Routledge, forthcoming 2012).

83 See, e.g., Lyon, '9/11, synopticon, and scopophilia'.

84 dana boyd, 'Dear voyeur, meet flaneur, sincerely, social media', *Surveillance and Society* 8: 4 (2011): 505–7.

85 Eli Pariser, *The Filter Bubble: What the Internet Is Hiding from You* (New York: Penguin, 2011).

86 Oscar Gandy, 'Consumer protection in cyberspace', *Triple C* 9: 2 (2011): 175–89.

87 There may be exceptions; I'm thinking here mainly of the surveillance context. Perhaps social media could be thought of in relation to Hardt and Negri's idea of the 'swarm' – also used by Bauman, e.g. in *Consuming Life* (Cambridge: Polity, 2007). See Michael Hardt and Antonio Negri, *Multitude: War and Democracy in the Age of Empire* (New York: Penguin, 2004). The use of social media during the so-called Arab Spring of 2011 appears to have some resonance with 'swarming'.

88 Jason Pridmore, 'Loyalty cards in the United States and Canada', in Elia Zureik et al., eds, *Surveillance, Privacy and the Globalization of Personal Information* (Montreal: McGill-Queen's University Press, 2010), p. 299.

89 Stephen Graham, 'Cities and the "war on terror"', *International Journal of Urban and Regional Research* 30: 2 (2006): 271.

90 James Der Derian, *Virtuous War: Mapping the Military-Industrial-Media-Entertainment Complex* (Boulder: Westview, 2001).

91 Which is a point made, slightly differently, by Bauman in *Consuming Life*.

Chapter 6

92 Gary T. Marx, 'An ethics for the new surveillance', *Information Society* 14: 3 (1998).

93 Gary T. Marx, *Undercover: Police Surveillance in America* (Berkeley: University of California Press, 1988), ch. 8.

94 Deleuze, 'Postscript'; David Garland, *The Culture of Control* (Chicago: University of Chicago Press, 2001).

95 N. Katherine Hayles, *How We Became Posthuman: Virtual Bodies in Cybernetics, Literature and Mathematics* (Chicago: University of Chicago Press, 1998), ch. 3.

96 Irma van der Ploeg, *The Machine-Readable Body* (Maastricht: Shaker, 2005), p. 94.

97 See, further, David Lyon, *Identifying Citizens: ID Cards as Surveillance* (Cambridge: Polity, 2009), pp. 124–5.

98 See Bauman, *Consuming Life*, pp. 14, 17–20.

99 Lucas Introna, 'The face and the interface: thinking with Levinas on ethics and justice in an electronically mediated world', working paper, Centre for the Study of Technology and Organization, University of Lancaster, 2003.

Chapter 7

100 Peter Beilharz, ed., *The Bauman Reader* (Oxford: Blackwell, 2001), p. 334.

101 These ideas are prompted by Jan Assman, *Das kulturelle Gedächtnis* (Munich: Beck, 1992), cited by Miroslav Volf and William H. Katerberg, *The Future of Hope: Christian Tradition amid Modernity and Postmodernity* (Grand Rapids, MI: Eerdmans, 2004), p. x.

102 This series was later published as Jacques Derrida, *Adieu à Emmanuel Levinas* (Paris: Galilée, 1997) and *Adieu to Emmanuel Levinas* (Stanford: Stanford University Press, 1999).

103 Robert Paul Doede and Edward Hughes, 'Wounded vision and the optics of hope', in Volf and Katerberg, *The Future of Hope*, p. 189.

104 Ibid., p. 193.

105 See 'Pour les enfants, Internet est aussi naturel que la mer ou la montagne', *Le Monde*, 30 Nov. 2011.

106 Pierre Bourdieu, *Distinction: A Social Critique of the Judgment of Taste* (London: Routledge, 1986), pp. 480–1.

107 Miroslav Volf, *Exclusion and Embrace: A Theological Exploration of Identity, Otherness and Reconciliation* (Nashville: Abingdon Press, 1996), p. 75.

108 Ibid., p. 277.
109 Ibid., p. 306.
110 Kieran Flanagan, 'Bauman's implicit theology', in Davis and Tester, *Bauman's Challenge*, p. 93.
111 'Tony Judt: "I am not pessimistic in the very long run"', *Independent*, 24 Mar. 2010.
112 Evan R. Goldstein, 'The trials of Tony Judt', *Chronicle Review*, 6 Jan.

Index

Index

Index

Index

Index

Index

Index

privacy 13
  and the internet 19, 21, 26
  and secrecy 27–8
proper distance 95–6
Psalm 139
  and the ethics of care 138–9,
    140
public services
  decline of investment in
    155–6

QR (quick response) codes 9,
  10

rationality
  and panopticons 57–8
reason
  and the ethics of surveillance
    139
  and modernity 80, 82
refugees
  and the banoptican 63,
    64–6
relationships see digitally
    mediated relationships
religion
  agency and hope 151–3
  religious confessions 26, 27
Renaissance ideas of peace and
    prosperity 118–19
resistance
  and the banopticon 62
responsibility 156–7
  'floating' of 94
RFIDs (radiofrequency
    identification) chips 9–10
Rhodes, Lorna 54, 56
Richtel, Matt 87, 89
risk
  calculation/management
    97–8, 99, 101

and insecurity 106–7
  and liquid modernity 145
Rose, Josh 25, 38, 40
Rousseau, JeanJacques 139
Rwanda 151

scopophilia
  and consumerist surveillance
    127–8
Second World War 86
secrecy and privacy 27–8
security
  and discipline 5, 107
  fear of security devices 105,
    106
  insecurity and surveillance
    100–20
  maintaining 100–1
Shakespeare, William
  Hamlet 100, 103
Shanker, Thom 19, 87, 89
Shannon, Claude 134
shopping malls 92
Silverstone, Roger 95–6, 98
Simmel, Georg 26
smartphones 4, 5, 9
social change
  Houellebecq on 109–10
social control ('Big Brother') 8,
    10–11, 12
social democracy 155
social exclusion 92–3
social media 18
  and anonymity 14
  and the confessional society
    28–30
  and consumerist surveillance
    127
  and digitally mediated
    relationships 35–7
  and exclusion 23–4

Index